PORTRAITS AND PAINTERS OF THE GOVERNORS OF INDIANA 1800–1978

by
Wilbur D. Peat

revised, edited and with new entries by
Diane Gail Lazarus
Indianapolis Museum of Art

Biographies of the governors by
Lana Ruegamer
Indiana Historical Society

Indiana Historical Society
Indianapolis Museum of Art
1978

C. 2

Credits:
Design: Nancy Singleton
Photography: Robert Wallace
Printing: Hilltop Press
Paper: 80 lb. Warren Cameo Dull
Cover: Weyerhaeuser—Torino Duo
Typesetting: Weimer Typesetting Co., Inc.
Type: Goudy Oldstyle

FOREWORD

IN THE SPRING of 1977, Governor Otis R. Bowen, M.D., appointed a special committee which was charged with recommending a restoration program for the Governors Portrait Collection, developing a suitable mechanism for future maintenance and augmentation of the collection, and studying ways in which the collection's full potential as a cultural, historical, and educational tool could be realized. The appointment of the Committee was occasioned in part by the passage of a House resolution introduced by Representative Robert W. Gordon, Connersville.

As a result of the Committee's efforts a contract was arranged in October, 1977, between the Department of Administration, State of Indiana, and the Indianapolis Museum of Art, for a program of restoration and documentation of the collection at the Indianapolis Museum of Art Conservation Laboratory.

In addition, the committee recommended that the Historical Bureau be given statutory responsibility for maintaining the collection. The 1978 General Assembly established that responsibility by passing Public Law No. 18 (IC 4-23-7-14.5).

Members of the Governors Portrait Collection Committee are Mr. Carl Armstrong, Director, Division of Historic Preservation, Department of Natural Resources, State of Indiana; Mr. William Du Bois, Executive Assistant to Governor Bowen; Miss Janet I. Harris, Executive Director, Indiana Arts Commission; Mr. James B. Kessler, Consultant, Budget Agency; Mrs. Clarence W. Long, Indianapolis; Mr. John J. Newman, State Archivist; Mr. James W. Sexson, Director, Property Management, Department of Administration; Mr. Robert A. Yassin, Director, Indianapolis Museum of Art. Mr. Martin Radecki, Chief Conservator, Indianapolis Museum of Art, has acted most ably as technical consultant.

Pamela J. Bennett, Director
Indiana Historical Bureau
State of Indiana

Portraits and Painters of the Governors
of Indiana
1800–1943
The Collection

(Reprinted from the 1944 publication)

FOR MORE than seventy years the state of Indiana has been collecting paintings. It has not acquired masterpieces of such rarity and worth as to arouse the jealousy of museum officials, but it has assembled in the State House a notable group of portraits. There are forty canvases, the likenesses of thirty-seven of the thirty-eight men who have served as chief executive of Indiana since it was made a territory. There are two pictures of three of the governors, Jennings, Morton, and Thomas A. Hendricks. Except for the portrait of John Gibson, who was acting governor of the territory on two occasions and is included in our list of chief executives, the roster is complete to date.

At present the portraits are displayed in the corridors on the fourth floor of the State House and in two of the executive offices where they may be seen at any time. People throughout the state are aware of their existence but unfortunately few seem impressed with the scope or historical significance of the collection. Part of this indifference may be due to the meager information which is available about the paintings, as well as to the poor lighting and unsatisfactory places for their display. The intrusion of office equipment into the corridors in recent years has added nothing to their effectiveness.

A label attached to the frame of each portrait gives the name of the subject and his term as chief executive. It does not carry, of course, the name of the artist nor the date of the painting, leaving people to conclude that each was painted from life when the man was occupying the governor's chair. Recent investigation has shown that such was not the case. Only thirteen of the portraits, to the best of our knowledge, were made during the incumbency of the subject; the others deviate from the men's terms in office by as little as a year or as much as a century, depending upon the obstacles encountered in securing adequate likenesses.

A collection of this kind is important for several reasons. Primarily it is a historical record or chronicle: it preserves the appearance, and to a certain extent the personality of each of Indiana's chief executives, and, being a collection of large paintings, it lends dignity and distinction to their office. As some of the portraits are the only known likenesses of the men, their documentary value is considerable.

But the collection is significant for another reason. It is more than an assemblage of faces. It represents the work of more than a dozen painters who lived and worked in Indiana at different times, and while some of them are not very well known today, others are ranked as our foremost artists. With the growing interest in American art, particularly that of the frontier regions, more attention is being given to the men who, however humbly, contributed to the rise of a native movement.

The value of the collection to people interested in this phase of the subject depends, quite naturally, upon their knowing who made the portraits and when the work was done. Until lately this information was not accessible: most of it had been forgotten or filed away in archives. Recent studies, however, have brought a good deal of it to light, enabling us now to identify the authors—fifteen in all—date the paintings more or less accurately, and reconstruct the history of each portrait. The following sketches are the outcome of this investigation.

It is not generally known that Governor Conrad Baker was responsible for starting the collection. In 1869 he began to assemble pictures that would "convey to future generations an idea of how the early rulers of Indiana looked."[1] Not satisfied with photographs or daguerreotypes, he undertook the arduous task of getting oil paintings. Seventeen men had preceded him as chief executive of the territory and state, and realizing that delay would only add to the difficulty of securing their portraits, he enlisted the help of the legislature and obtained its authorization at the special session of 1869 "to secure, as soon as practicable, a true and life-like likeness of each of the Governors of the State and Territory of Indiana, including the present incumbent, to be placed in the State Library," at a cost not exceeding two hundred dollars each.[2] Then he called upon people in different parts of the state to help him find pictures which

---

[1] Quoted in a letter from James Forbes to John M. Commons, Governor Baker's private secretary, October 11, 1869. Governor Baker's correspondence, folder relating to governors' portraits, Archives Division, Indiana State Library, hereafter cited as Governor Baker's correspondence.

[2] *Laws of Indiana,* 1869 (special session), p. 11.

could be acquired or borrowed as models for artists to copy. His next step was that of selecting the painters for the different portraits—a task which might have been very difficult if he had not already given some thought to the matter, and if he had not counted among his friends several of the local painters.

The sustained interest of Governor Baker and his friends brought about the desired results within a few months, and the foundation of the official portrait gallery was laid. Six artists were employed on the project at the time, working from living models or from earlier paintings or photographs as the circumstances required. Their work seems to have satisfied the governor and met the specifications of the legislature. Each portrait presented a different problem, as the following pages show. Thirteen of the seventeen preceding governors had died, making the job of obtaining likenesses a difficult one—some had died before the introduction of photography. The portraits of the men who were still living in 1869 presented no serious obstacles.

Since Baker's administration, the collection has grown steadily, each governor posing for his portrait before an artist of his choice, either during his term in office or soon after. Upon acceptance, the portraits have been hung in the State House and placed under the custody of the Indiana State Library. Since 1927 their procurement has been directed by the Indiana Historical Bureau, while the amount appropriated by the legislature has been increased to five hundred dollars in most cases.

For the sake of clarity the following discussion of the individual portraits is based on the chronology of the administrations rather than on the dates of the individual paintings. For instance, the earliest paintings in the group, made about 1835–1840, are the likenesses of James Brown Ray, governor from 1822 to 1831 and Noah Noble, governor from 1831 to 1837, while the portrait of William Henry Harrison, the first governor, was not painted until 1869. . . .

Wilbur D. Peat, 1944

Editor's Introduction and Acknowledgments

IN HIS introduction to the 1944 publications, Wilbur D. Peat made clear the significance of the Indiana governors portrait collection. His admirable catalogue identifying historic materials related to the collection and documenting the circumstances of the commissions was a great contribution to our knowledge of this major body of work. Around the time of Peat's publication the portrait collection was suffering from disinterest and neglect in its general condition and method of display. Not much attention has been paid to the collection since that time aside from a minor restoration project in 1953 and an occasional rehanging of a few portraits at the discretion of the incumbent governor. The 1978 conservation treatment of the portraits and the updating and revision of the catalogue mark a new level of interest in the collection which will result in its preservation for the enjoyment of future generations of Indiana's citizens.

The state has now been collecting paintings for one hundred and ten years. In the thirty-five years since Peat's publication, eight governors' portraits have been added to the collection introducing seven new governors and seven different artists. (The portrait of Henry Frederick Schricker in this group is the second portrait of this governor, painted in his second term; it is also the second portrait by Randolph Coats.) Each additional portrait is represented by a catalogue entry in this revised, updated edition of *Portraits and Painters of the Governors of Indiana*. Also, in the current reinstallation of the collection, the "epochal" governors' portraits painted by Theodore Clement Steele in 1916—Harrison, Jennings, Morton and Thomas A. Hendricks, will hang together in the executive offices. This brings the number of paintings in the official collection to forty-nine.

The 1944 catalogue was revised following several guidelines. First, new information which had come to light since Peat's initial research on the collection necessitated major revisions in some cases. Also, conservation treatment, particularly cleaning and the removal of yellowed varnish, changed the appearance of several of the portraits, and adjustments in the descriptions of paintings were made accordingly. Changes in stylistic analysis were made only in cases where additional comments would provide continuity or context.

* * * *

THERE ARE several persons who must be acknowledged for their contributions to this project. To the staff of the Library, Indiana Historical Society, and to Joseph Zywicki, Chief Curator, and Teresa Cruz, Registrar, Chicago Historical Society, the editor is extremely grateful for so much able assistance with research questions. Martin Radecki, David Miller, and Monica Radecki, Conservators, Indianapolis Museum of Art, provided valuable insight during the conservation treatment of the paintings; Vanessa Wicker, Associate Registrar, Indianapolis Museum of Art, assisted with research on the artists' biographies; Robert Wallace, Photographer, Indianapolis Museum of Art, was responsible for the superb photographs and color transparencies reproduced in this book; and Janet Feemster, Curatorial Secretary, Indianapolis Museum of Art, cheerfully turned my research notes and drafts into clean copy. Thanks are also extended to Pamela J. Bennett, Director, Indiana Historical Bureau, for her guidance through the various stages of the project, and to Mary Jane Meeker, Researcher, Indiana Historical Bureau, with whom the editor worked closely in research. Finally, special thanks are reserved for Robert A. Yassin, Director, Indianapolis Museum of Art, who served as my editor, reading the manuscript, making so many valuable suggestions which have been incorporated in this book, and seeing the publication through the press.

The editor is also grateful to the late Wilbur D. Peat in whose footsteps it is always inspiring to follow.

Diane Gail Lazarus
Indianapolis Museum of Art, 1978

A Note on the Biographies

BIOGRAPHICAL sketches of the governors have been added to this newly revised edition of *Portraits and Painters of the Governors of Indiana* in order to serve two purposes. First, it is hoped that the sketches will fill a need in Indiana history for a readable introduction to the governors themselves and serve as a handy reference tool. And second, it was believed that the sketches, suggesting something of the careers and personalities of the subjects, would add to the impact of the portraits.

The sketches have been composed with an aim to suggest what the men who have been Indiana's governors were like—not to evaluate their performances as governor. Their administrations have been characterized only briefly in the following pages, mentioning but a few areas of concern and/or major accomplishments in each administration. Each sketch focuses on the family, education, and career of a governor and attempts, in addition, to suggest something of the individuality of the man.

The most useful sources for information about the governors were the following: Hazel Hopper (comp.), "Indiana," in Robert Sobel and John Raimo (eds.), *Biographical Directory of the Governors of the United States 1789–1978* (4 volumes, Westport, Conn., 1978), I, 395–425; *Dictionary of American Biography;* and the Biography Index and Governors' newspaper files of the Indiana Division, Indiana State Library.

Lana Ruegamer, Editor,
assisted by
Paula J. Corpuz, Editor, and
Lisa Nowak, Editorial Assistant,
Indiana Historical Society

Editor's Note:

THE MATERIAL for this publication has been arranged following Wilbur Peat's order, that is, chronologically according to the years of the governor's administration. For each governor the information has been divided into two parts: a biographical sketch of the governor, followed by a discussion of his portrait and the artist who painted it.

In the catalogue information provided for the paintings of each governor, an asterisk (*) following the artist's nationality listed as "American" indicates that the artist was born or lived in Indiana and is considered to be a member of the Indiana school.

A "c." before a date indicates that the date is approximate. Two dates separated by a slash (/) means that the work was executed at some time within the given time period. Two dates separated by a hyphen (-) means that the work was begun and completed over the indicated period of time.

Dimensions are given in inches, height before width, followed in parentheses by the same dimensions in centimeters.

All inscriptions are taken from the front only: "l.r." indicates *lower right,* "u.l." indicates *upper left,* and so on.

William Henry Harrison, 1773–1841
Governor May 13, 1800–December 28, 1812

WILLIAM HENRY HARRISON was born in Virginia, the son of Benjamin Harrison, who was himself a governor of Virginia and one of the signers of the Declaration of Independence. Educated at Hampden-Sidney College, the young Harrison entered medical school but was forced to leave in 1791 when his father died. From 1792 to 1794 Harrison was Anthony Wayne's aide-de-camp in battles against the Miami Indians, and he was promoted to captain in 1797.

Harrison was appointed secretary of the Northwest Territory on June 26, 1798, and in 1799 was elected a territorial delegate to Congress, where he served until May, 1800, when he was appointed governor of the Indiana Territory, an area that initially included all of the original Northwest Territory except Ohio. The twenty-seven-year-old Harrison was to serve as governor of Indiana Territory for twelve years. His dual responsibilities to secure justice for the Indians and to acquire Indian land were often contradictory, but his administration was generally able and honest. With full powers of appointment to office, Harrison was conscientious in seeking out local recommendations for appointees and encouraging the development of representative government in the new territory. During his governorship his military career was enhanced when he defeated the Prophet at Tippecanoe in 1811. He was given command of the Army of the Northwest in the fall of 1812 and resigned as governor a few months later. His forces decisively defeated the British at the Battle of the Thames in 1813.

Harrison served as representative to Congress from Ohio from 1816 to 1819, and was elected to one term in the Ohio legislature in 1819. In 1825 he was sent to the United States Senate from the same state. He served as minister to Colombia from 1828 to 1829. Harrison ran for President as a Whig in 1836 and was defeated by Martin Van Buren, but he was victorious in the 1840 race. Harrison died on April 4, 1841, one month after his inauguration, the shortest term of any President in American history.

Harrison, sometimes described as the "Washington of the West," was the grandfather of the twenty-third President of the United States, Benjamin Harrison.

* * * *

WILLIAM HENRY HARRISON sat for his portrait on several occasions,[3] but evidently no painting made from life could be procured when Governor Baker was assembling the collection. A copy or replica of another portrait had to be made, and Barton S. Hays, a well-known Indianapolis artist during the

sixties and seventies, was selected to do the work. He was an Ohioan by birth but had come to Indiana as a youth, settling in Montgomery County and embarking upon his career by making likenesses of relatives and friends in Wingate, Covington, and Attica—frequently for his room and board. Like most of Indiana's early painters he found portraiture more remunerative than landscape painting, and, although he had very little formal training, he developed into a very capable technician. His residence in Indianapolis dated from 1858, at which time he established a Daguerrean firm with a man named Runnion. Within a few years he acquired a good reputation working either from photographs (a very popular method in those days) or from life. It is reported that at the time he was receiving seventy-five dollars for a portrait showing the head and shoulders and one hundred dollars if it included the hands.

When the commissions for the portraits of the governors were being given in 1869, Hays was one of the leading painters in Indianapolis, and it is not surprising to learn that he was asked to make the Harrison portrait. Unfortunately no records have been found describing its evolution. Since Hays had to rely on another picture, he probably selected one which was most convincing in its likeness and characterization, as well as concurrent in date with Harrison's term in office. A comparative study of the known portraits of Harrison leads to the conclusion that Hays copied an oil portrait which is now in the collection of Bowdoin College Museum of Art.[4] The pose, costume, lighting, and age of the subject in the two paintings are almost identical, as is the size of the canvases.

Hays succeeded in making a very forceful portrait of Harrison. It is a good likeness and an unusually convincing character study. Harrison's expression is resolute and tense; a look of incisiveness, and not a little shrewdness, appears in the eyes and about the mouth; the forms of the head are strongly and fully modeled. Some of the picture's strength comes from its rich, deep colors;

---

[3] Among the artists who painted William Henry Harrison are Thomas Sully, Rembrandt Peale, Henry Inman, J. R. Lambdin, and Bass Otis.

[4] Unknown artist, *William Henry Harrison,* c. 1850, oil on canvas, 36 x 26, Gift of Allison Owen of Cincinnati, Bowdoin College Museum of Art, 1870. If the Bowdoin portrait was in Cincinnati until about 1870 as the credit line and accession number would have one believe, then Hays may have painted his copy directly from the original in 1869. It is likely, however, that Hays copied the portrait from a photograph, a method with which he was very familiar, or from one of the several engravings of the Bowdoin portrait. See the notebook on William Henry Harrison portraits compiled by Arthur J. Mitten, Indiana Historical Society.

1
WILLIAM HENRY HARRISON, 1869
Barton Stone Hays, American*, 1826–1914
oil on canvas, 36¼ x 29¼ (92.0 x 74.4)
Unsigned

ruddy flesh tones and deep blacks are placed against a greenish-gray background, and red accents appear at the left where light falls on the upholstery of the chair.

For some years there was a copy of the Hays portrait of Harrison in the State House collection made by T. C. Steele in 1916. This was Indiana's centennial year, and Samuel Ralston, then governor, asked Steele to paint the portraits of four governors who belonged to "epochal" periods of the state's history. They were Harrison, first territorial governor, Jennings, first state governor, Morton, the Civil War governor, and Thomas A. Hendricks, an outstanding figure in the period of development following that war. For the Harrison portrait Steele is reported to have used "prints that had been handed down through past generations as authoritative."[5] The artist's own inscription on the front of the painting contradicts this assertion. It reads: "After the library portrait, T. C. Steele." The paintings of the governors were always referred to as the library portraits because they hung in the State Library when it was in the State House. Even if this inscription were not on the canvas, a comparison of the two would convince one that Steele copied the painting by Hays.

The "epochal" portraits by T. C. Steele are a part of the official collection and have throughout their history been disbursed and hung in historic homes of the state. As a result of the interest in the collection inspired by the 1978 conservation treatment, the four epochal portraits will be hung together in the State House.

---

[5] *Indianapolis News*, May 20, 1916, p. 17, col. 1.

John Gibson, 1740–1822
Acting Governor July 4, 1800–January 10, 1801
June, 1812–May,1813

JOHN GIBSON was born and raised in Lancaster, Pennsylvania. In 1758 he served in the Forbes expedition against the French at Fort Duquesne, remaining at Fort Pitt after the war as an Indian trader. At the outbreak of Pontiac's rebellion Gibson was captured and rescued from death when an old squaw whose son was slain in battle adopted him. For several years Gibson remained with the Indians in southwest Virginia, learning their language and customs, and he allegedly married a sister of Logan, the Mingo warrior. In 1764 he was released and returned to Fort Pitt. Ten years later he participated in Dunmore's War and was the translator for the written account of Chief Logan's famous speech, suing for peace. ("I appeal to any white man to say if he ever entered Logan's cabin hungry and he gave him not meat. . . .")

During the early stages of the Revolutionary War Gibson was active in Indian negotiations; later he fought under Washington, eventually commanding his own regiment. After the war he was an Allegheny County judge, major-general of the militia, and a member of Pennsylvania's constitutional convention in 1790. Thomas Jefferson appointed the sixty-year-old Gibson secretary of the Indiana Territory in 1800, in which office he served until 1816.

Although Gibson is known as Indiana's second territorial governor, he was really only acting governor during William Henry Harrison's absences. After the state government was formed in 1816, the elderly Gibson returned to Pennsylvania.

****

A DOCUMENTED portrait of John Gibson has not been found to date, although numerous attempts have been made to find one. Over the years several portraits have been associated with this governor's name. Conrad Baker had written to John B. Dillon, historian, in 1869 about the possibility of obtaining portraits of certain men, among them Gibson, and Dillon replied that he doubted the existence of a contemporary likeness of the territorial secretary.[6] Baker continued his search during his administration, and other attempts were made in later years to supply the missing picture. A portrait believed to be of Gibson was published in the *Indianapolis News* late in 1932 in connection with a series of articles about the governors of Indiana,[7] but later investigation disclosed that the portrait was not that of the Secretary of Indiana Territory but a contemporary Pennsylvanian of the same name.

In 1941, another painting surfaced which was said to be a portrait of John Gibson.[8] In April of that year, Mrs. Marguerite Anderson of the Indiana Division of the State Library received an inquiry from a Mrs. Marie Carey of New York regarding the career of John Gibson. In the correspondence that followed, the Library learned that Mrs. Carey owned a portrait of John Gibson which, she wrote, had come into her possession through several relatives from Gibson's daughter. The painter was unknown, but an inscription[9] on the reverse of the canvas indicated that the portrait was painted in Philadelphia in 1806. The portrait was in poor condition, dark and colorless. In the interest of historical documentation, Eli Lilly of Indianapolis purchased the portrait and it currently hangs in Grouseland, the Vincennes home of William Henry Harrison. It was included in Wilbur Peat's catalogue, *Portraits and Painters of the Governors of Indiana* of 1944. This portrait was copied by an Indiana artist for the official collection in 1964.[10]

The discovery of this painting in 1941 would certainly have provided a satisfying conclusion to a long, frustrating search to complete the official collection. Unfortunately, a shadow of doubt was cast upon the authenticity of the Gibson portrait in 1947 by an unrelated inquiry into the affairs of a dealer of questionable repute, a Mrs. Collins,[11] of New York. Mrs. Collins used several aliases, among them "Mrs. Carey." She corresponded with many institutions from the address given by Mrs. Carey in her letters to the Indiana State Library

---

6 Dillon to Governor Baker, August 16, 1869. Governor Baker's correspondence.

7 *Indianapolis News*, November 30, 1932, part 2, p.1.

8 See *Indiana History Bulletin*, XIX, no. 4, April, 1942, p. 150, and Wilbur D. Peat, *Portraits and Painters of the Governors of Indiana*, Indianapolis, Indiana Historical Society, 1944, pp. 392–93 for more information.

9 The inscription on the back of the canvas, written in ink by an unknown hand, reads, *Judge John Gibson Indian Interpreter & Judge of Allegheny County. Portrait June 1806 Phila. Given to his daughter Mrs. George Wallace.* The inscription was reported by Peat, *loc. cit.* It was covered in relining the canvas in 1941.

10 David Mannweiler, " 'Lost' Portrait Fills Out Set," *Indianapolis News*, January 13, 1978, reports the circumstances of the copy.

11 G. William Berquist, Reference Department, The New York Public Library, to Howard Peckham, Director, Indiana Historical Bureau, May 6, 1947. The original has been lost, but copies of the letter exist in the files of the Indiana Historical Bureau and Indiana Historical Society.

2
JOHN GIBSON
(No portrait)

regarding the Gibson portrait. It seems that she had sold and offered many portraits of an historical nature which were not what they purported to be. This information does not prove the Gibson portrait to be unauthentic, but it does raise grave suspicions. It is to be hoped that some future technical examination of the portrait will bring more conclusive information to light.

Thomas Posey, 1750–1818
Governor March 3, 1813–November 7, 1816

THOMAS POSEY was born in Virginia and educated in the country schools. An adventurer and a soldier, he began his military career at age nineteen fighting with a Virginia company against the Indians. He served with distinction during the American Revolution and settled down in Spottsylvania County for a few years afterward to serve as county lieutenant and magistrate.

He joined Anthony Wayne in fighting the Indian wars in the Northwest for a year, and then he moved to Kentucky, where he served in the state senate and as lieutenant governor. Moving with the frontier, General Posey turned up in Louisiana by 1812 and briefly served as United States senator from that state. He was appointed governor of the Indiana Territory in 1813 following Harrison's resignation and served in that capacity until statehood in 1816.

He ran unsuccessfully for governor against Jonathan Jennings in 1816 and was appointed Indian agent for Illinois Territory. He died in Shawneetown while serving in the office.

Handsome and graceful, distinguished by a military bearing, Posey was believed by some to have been George Washington's natural son.

* * * *

THE PORTRAIT of Thomas Posey was painted at the time Governor Baker was ordering the work for the State House. A clue to the whereabouts of an authentic likeness of Posey came through a picture of him in Dillon's *History of Indiana.* [12] Upon writing to the author in Washington for information about the original picture, Governor Baker was referred to relatives of Posey in Kentucky. They owned a miniature of him painted in 1795 by the noted American artist, James Peale (1749–1831). [13]

The man selected to copy and enlarge this miniature for the state was John Bayless Hill, a young local artist. "Jackie" Hill, as he was familiarly called, was born in Indianapolis in 1849, the son of John F. Hill of the firm of Drum and Hill. He studied for a brief period with Jacob Cox, the leading painter of the city. [14] He was introduced to Governor Baker by A. H. Conner, proprietor of the *Indianapolis Daily and Weekly Journal,* as "an artist of rare promise." [15] However, Hill's connection with Cox was probably more of a recommendation than Conner's letter, since we have reason to believe that Governor Baker and Jacob Cox were close friends. Hill was only twenty when the collection was being formed, but he had a studio of his own and must have been regarded as a portraitist of sufficient ability to carry out the order. [16]

A comparison of Hill's painting with a photograph of the miniature shows that he took a number of liberties with the original. Thomas Posey appears younger—much too young if we want to think of the portrait as representing him while in office—and his handsome, boyish face is decidedly lacking in character and expression. It is regrettable that no portrait exists depicting Posey as a man approaching sixty-three, his age at the time he became governor of Indiana Territory. He had fought in the Revolution and with Wayne in the Northwest and had risen to the rank of major-general. His ripe years and wide experience must have given him a forceful appearance, hardly like that which confronts us in the State House portrait.

John Hill's method of working was precise and painstaking. The brush strokes lack decisiveness and the paint is thin. The colors are peculiar, [17] too; the pale background, mottled with rose and gray tints, seems to emphasize the gentle, wistful character of the subject.

---

[12] John B. Dillon, *A History of Indiana...*, Indianapolis, 1859, frontispiece.

[13] Wilbur Peat states that the Posey miniature (present location unknown) was painted by Rembrandt Peale (1778–1860) in 1795, but this attribution is a mistake. A photograph of the miniature in the Indiana Picture Collection, Governors' File, Indiana State Library, bears an inscription assigning the miniature to Rembrandt Peale's uncle, the well-known miniature painter James Peale (1749–1831). From what can be determined by the photograph, the style of painting bears out this attribution. Furthermore, in 1795, when the miniature was most likely painted, Rembrandt Peale was seventeen years of age, and James Peale was at the height of his career as a miniature painter.

[14] Jacob P. Dunn, *Greater Indianapolis...* 2 volumes, Chicago, 1910, I, 482.

[15] Conner to Governor Baker, July 29, 1869. Governor Baker's correspondence.

[16] See Wilbur D. Peat, *Pioneer Painters of Indiana,* Art Association of Indianapolis, Indiana, 1954, pp. 180, 195, 233, for further information on John B. Hill.

[17] Hill's use of color was not related to the miniature, if one is to take as fact the inscription on the photograph cited in note 13, above. The description of color reads as follows: *Eyes blue; hair chestnut; color, florid:/coat lead grey, vest black satin.*

3
THOMAS POSEY, 1869
John Bayless Hill, American*, 1849–1874
oil on canvas, 30⅛ x 26³/₁₆ (76.5 x 65.6)
Unsigned

Jonathan Jennings, 1784–1834
Governor November 7, 1816–September 12, 1822

JONATHAN JENNINGS, Indiana's first state governor, was a minister's son, born in New Jersey and educated in the common schools of Pennsylvania. Like most of his successors in the governor's chair, Jennings was a lawyer.

He was elected as territorial delegate to Congress in 1809, 1811, 1812, and 1814, and served as president of the convention called to frame a constitution for the new state of Indiana. His politics were of a personal rather than a party nature. Jennings was elected governor in 1816, handily defeating the incumbent territorial governor, Thomas Posey. He served two terms, leaving office in 1822 after his election to Congress, to which he was re-elected in 1824, 1826, and 1828. He also served on commissions in 1818 and 1832 to negotiate treaties with the Potawatomi, Wea, and Miami Indians. Indiana historian William Wesley Woollen says that Jennings lost his seat in Congress in 1830 because his friends were concerned about his drinking problem, believing that life in Washington tended to increase Jennings's dependence on alcohol.

Jennings had blue eyes, a fair complexion, and sandy hair. He was about five feet eight and one half inches tall, and later in his life he tended to corpulence. Woollen describes Jennings as "a man of polished manners . . . he was always gentle and kind to those about him. He was not an orator, but he could tell what he knew in a pleasing way. He wrote well, as well perhaps as any of his successors in the Governor's office."

* * * *

THE SIGNATURE which appears on the portrait of Jonathan Jennings has an unfamiliar ring to students of Indiana art. Dunn says, in writing of the governors' portraits: "there had been a Canadian painter, James Forbes, who visited Evansville, and painted a portrait of John B. Baker, brother of Governor Baker, and impressed the Governor with his ability as an artist. Nothing is known of Forbes here beyond his work, and the fact that he was a typical Englishman in appearance and dress. Governor Baker had Forbes paint his own portrait, and also the portraits of Governors Jennings, Whitcomb, Dunning and Morton."[18] To these should be added the name of Governor Boon.

It is surprising to learn that a stranger was commissioned to paint so many of the official portraits, and that his visit was so shrouded in mystery that no one was able to give a report of him after he left Indianapolis. It is known that his name was brought to Governor Baker's attention by H. F. Blount, of Evansville, who wrote to the Governor about his work, adding: "I should be glad if he might be favorably remembered in the selection of an artist."[19] Forbes had returned to Chicago and Baker wrote to him there asking if he would consider painting certain of the governors. Forbes replied that he would, and in the correspondence that followed he expounded some of his theories on portrait painting but, unfortunately, said nothing about his career as an artist.[20]

Contrary to Dunn's statement, James Forbes was a Scotsman, not a Canadian. He was born in Scotland about 1800, and before emigrating had received training in his native land, and had exhibited paintings at the Royal Scottish Academy and at the Royal Academy, London. It is not known when he came to America, but he had a studio in Chicago after 1860.[21] Dunn's reference to him as a Canadian suggests that he lived in Canada prior to coming to Chicago, but this has not been verified. After completing his commissions for Indiana nothing more was heard of him here; even the date and place of his death have not been determined.

As no original portrait of Jonathan Jennings could be purchased by the state in 1869, it was again necessary to find a picture for Forbes to copy. It is well established that he used a miniature which Jennings brought as a present to Ann Hay, his fiancee, upon his return from his first year as Indiana's delegate in Congress.[22] Forbes has effectively captured the spirit of the original, yet he has worked so broadly that his version does not reveal its derivation from a miniature. The artist has extended the portrait to include the hands and upper torso. Since the original was painted about 1810, the Forbes painting makes Jennings look younger than he actually was during his administration. He appears as a dapper young man, stylish in dress, with a forthright, intelligent face. The colors are subdued, and, although they do not conform with descriptions of the subject's coloration, they give the portrait a rich effect.

Jonathan Jennings was the second "epochal"

[18] Dunn, Greater Indianapolis, I, 481.

[19] Blount to Governor Baker, July 7, 1869. Governor Baker's correspondence.

[20] Forbes to Governor Baker, July 20 and 29, August 6, and September 1, 1869. Ibid.

[21] Ulrich Thieme and Felix Becker (eds.), Allgemeines Lexikon der bildenden Künstler . . ., Leipsig, XII, 1916, p. 201.

[22] Mabel C. Morrison, Ann Gilmore Hay, Wife of Jonathan Jennings from 1811 to 1826, Indianapolis, 1925, p. 12; see also p. 20 for a reproduction of the picture from which Forbes worked. A photograph of the miniature is in the Picture Collection, Indiana State Library.

JONATHAN JENNINGS, 1869
James Forbes, American, b. Scotland, c. 1800–?
Oil on canvas, 36 x 29 (91.5 x 73.6)
Signed l.l.: Jas. Forbes/Pinxt

Governor whom T. C. Steele painted for Samuel Ralston in 1916, so there are two portraits of him in the State House. These are so similar that it is reasonable to assume that Steele copied the one by Forbes or used a photograph of the miniature referred to above.

Ratliff Boon, 1781–1844
Governor September 12–December 5, 1822

RATLIFF BOON came to Warrick County, Indiana, from Kentucky in 1809. After attending public schools, Boon learned the gunsmith trade but soon began a long political career with his election as Warrick County treasurer in 1813. He then served as a member of the Indiana House of Representatives, the Indiana Senate, and in 1819 was elected lieutenant governor on the ticket with Jonathan Jennings. Upon Jennings's resignation as governor in September, 1822, Boon filled out the unexpired term.

Boon was again elected lieutenant governor in 1822 when William Hendricks was elected governor and served until January, 1824, when he decided to run for Congress. Elected as a staunch Jacksonian Democrat that year, he was unsuccessful in his bid for re-election in 1826, but was elected to the five succeeding Congresses, serving twelve years in all, 1825 to 1827, 1829 to 1839. In 1836 Boon was a candidate for the United States Senate but was defeated by Oliver H. Smith. He moved to Missouri in 1839 and took part also in the politics of that state. An acquaintance described Boon as a "lithe, active man when I last saw him. In height he was about five feet ten inches, spare in person, and as straight as an Indian. His forehead was low and receded rapidly from his eyebrows." Historian Will Fortune observed, "his education was limited, but he was a man of extraordinary tact and sagacity."

****

RATLIFF BOON is represented in the portrait collection by a painting which also bears the signature of James Forbes.[23] An inscription indicates that the painting was copied in 1870, but, due to an overcleaning or fading of the inscription, the source of the copy is no longer discernible. The search for the portrait which would serve as a model took place in 1869, twenty-five years after Boon's death and was directed toward Boonville, Indiana. Isaac S. Moore informed Governor Baker that John Hacpole of that town had a picture of "Mr. Boon said to be a good likeness of him,"[24] and evidently it was the one which Forbes copied. This may be the same portrait of Ratliff Boon which was obtained in Boonville at the time that the Corydon capitol building was being restored.[25] From this portrait Forbes succeeded in making a convincing likeness of his subject. The pose is quiet but not without the suggestion of vitality; the features are sensitively drawn and clean-cut; and Boon's expression is one of thoughtfulness as he gazes out into space. The colors are full-bodied: a black suit and a tawny face are set against a warm brown background, and a deep red note is made by the chair on the left side of the composition.

---

[23] This portrait is erroneously assigned to Jacob Cox by Dunn in *Greater Indianapolis*, I, 481.

[24] Moore to Governor Baker, September 22, 1869. Governor Baker's correspondence.

[25] The portrait of Ratliff Boon from which the Forbes portrait may be a copy is in the collection of the Indiana State Division of Historic Preservation and is currently housed at Corydon Capital State Memorial.

5
RATLIFF BOON, 1870
James Forbes, American, b. Scotland, c. 1800–?
oil on canvas, 36 x 29 (91.5 x 73.6)
Signed and dated l.r.: Jas. Forbes/Copied 1870/Original/18.?.

William Hendricks, 1782–1850
Governor December 5, 1822–February 12, 1825

WILLIAM HENDRICKS, born in Pennsylvania, was educated in a common school, read law, and was admitted to the bar in Cincinnati. In 1812 he came to Madison, Indiana Territory, where he practiced law and established the *Eagle*, the second newspaper published in Indiana. After only a few years in Madison he was elected to the territorial house of representatives and was secretary of the Indiana Constitutional Convention in 1816. A Democratic-Republican, Hendricks won election in August, 1816, as the first state representative to Congress from Indiana and was re-elected twice to this office.

Hendricks, running unopposed, was elected governor in 1822. It was during this term of office that the capital was moved from Corydon to Indianapolis. Hendricks resigned in 1825 upon election to the United States Senate. Re-elected to the Senate in 1830, Hendricks served until 1837, having been defeated for re-election by Oliver H. Smith in 1836. After twenty-one years in public office, he returned to Madison to practice law and manage his large estate.

Smith and Hendricks were friends, and Smith remembers him: "He had a smile on his face and a warm shake of the hand for all he met. He was not of the very first order of talents, but made all up by his plain, practical, good sense. He never attempted to speak upon subjects he did not understand." He was about six feet tall and had red hair and blue eyes. His nephew, Thomas A. Hendricks, was elected governor of Indiana in 1873.

* * * *

GOVERNOR WILLIAM HENDRICKS had an aversion to posing for artists during his lifetime, hence the procurement of his portrait posed the greatest problem for Governor Baker. The effort proved the determination with which the citizens of Indiana met the task of completing the official collection.

The first portrait of William Hendricks was in the collection for a very short time.[26] It was painted by a New Castle, Kentucky, lawyer, R. H. Buckley, an associate of Hendricks who professed to have been a painter in his youth. Buckley offered to paint the portrait from memory with the aid of a photograph of the governor's brother, Jamison Hendricks, a memory sketch by the governor's son, Grover, and verbal descriptions offered by William Hendricks's associates. Governor Baker was anxious to complete the project before his term expired, and, having exhausted all apparent possibilities, he commissioned Buckley to make the likeness. The painting was delivered in December, 1870, and was promptly removed from the collection three years later by Thomas A.

Hendricks when he assumed office in 1873, on the grounds that the portrait was not a true likeness of his uncle.

For almost fifty years there was no portrait of William Hendricks in the collection, and there is nothing to show that any definite steps were taken by officials to find one. In 1919, an H. J. Gensler of the Official Reporters' Office, United States Senate, made the fortuitous discovery of a picture of William Hendricks in a painting of a group of eighty-six Congressmen. Gensler identified Hendricks as the seventh figure from the lower left corner in Samuel F. B. Morse's painting, *The Old House of Representatives* of 1822, in the collection of the Corcoran Gallery of Art, Washington, D.C.

Plans were made to get a photograph of the diminutive figure, so that a local painter could make an enlarged oil copy, but several problems arose. Each individual pictured in the Morse painting actually sat for his portrait, but the artist's primary concern was to faithfully represent the National Hall,[27] consequently the features of Hendricks were not well defined. Also, the poor condition of the painting at the time rendered the photograph of the figure useless.

After several unsuccessful attempts were made to engage an artist to copy the portrait directly for the sum of money authorized by the state legislature, the matter was dropped. In 1925, through the efforts of the Indiana Historical Bureau and Merrill Moores, representing the Seventh Indiana District in Congress, a Washington artist, Samuel Burtis Baker, was commissioned to make an enlarged replica of William Hendricks from the Morse painting.

Baker, a portrait painter, was at the time Vice Principal and Instructor at the Corcoran School of Art and Adjunct Professor of Painting at the George Washington University. Born in Boston, Baker studied there with Joseph De Camp and taught in Cambridge, Massachusetts, at the Rindge School before going to Washington. He was a prolific and successful portrait painter in Washington, where he died in 1967.

---

[26] For a more detailed description of the events leading up to the acquisition of the Burtis Baker portrait of William Hendricks see the catalogue entry and footnotes for the portrait in Wilbur D. Peat, *Portraits and Painters of the Governors of Indiana*, 1944, pp. 397–400.

[27] The Corcoran Gallery of Art, Washington, D.C., *A Catalogue of the Collection of American Paintings in the Corcoran Gallery of Art*, Washington, D.C., Corcoran Gallery of Art, 1966, I, p. 53, illus. p. 52.

6
WILLIAM HENDRICKS, 1926
Samuel Burtis Baker, American, 1882–1967
oil on canvas, 32³/₁₆ x 26⁵/₁₆ (81.7 x 66.8)
Unsigned

Baker approached the project with a dual concern:[28] to remain faithful to Morse's picture of Hendricks; to make the necessary changes in the interest of an accurate likeness.[29] Guided by Merrill Moores, Baker consulted descriptions of William Hendricks in books and sought the advice of William Henry Smith, an "old newspaper man" living in Washington, who had been a close associate of Hendricks. On the authority of the above sources, Baker changed the hair color from black to sandy and made the background grey to relieve the hair. The eyes have been opened and have been made blue. To improve the total construction, the ear has been raised in keeping with the tilt of the head. Finally, the clothes have been drawn in greater detail in accord with the styles of the day. Baker has cleverly footnoted his major source by using Merrill Moores's copy of *Life and*

Public Services of Thomas A. Hendricks by Holcombe and Skinner as a model for the book in Hendricks's hand.

Stylistically, Baker has worked in a broad, direct manner. The generalized effect is appropriate since the portrait represents a synthesis of verbal reports and visual imagery, rather than a finished likeness.

[28] The following discussion of Baker's approach to the Hendricks portrait was explained by Baker in a letter of May 24, 1926, from Samuel Burtis Baker to C. Coleman, Director of the Indiana Historical Bureau. Governors' portraits files, Indiana Historical Bureau.

[29] For descriptions of William Hendricks used by Burtis Baker, see William Wesley Woollen, *Biographical and Historical Sketches of Early Indiana*, Indianapolis, Hammond & Co., 1883, pp. 54–55; and John Walker Holcombe and Hubert M. Skinner, *Life and Public Services of Thomas A. Hendricks with Selected Speeches and Writings*, Indianapolis, Carlon & Hollenbeck, 1886, p. 19.

James Brown Ray, 1794–1848
Governor February 12, 1825–December 7, 1831

JAMES BROWN RAY was born in Kentucky, studied law in Cincinnati, and moved to Brookville, Indiana, in 1818. In 1821 he was elected to the Indiana House of Representatives and in 1822 to the Indiana State Senate. When Ratliff Boon, the lieutenant governor, resigned in January, 1824, to run for Congress, Ray was elected president pro tempore of the state senate, and then Ray filled out the unexpired term of Governor William Hendricks when the latter was elected to the United States Senate in January, 1825. Ray was subsequently elected twice to his own terms as governor. He was quite young when first elected governor and was accused of being younger than the constitutionally required thirty years old. Ray was the last nonpartisan candidate to be elected governor in Indiana.

During Ray's administration the construction of the Michigan Road and the Wabash and Erie Canal was undertaken, and Ray served as a commissioner to negotiate treaties with the Potawatomi and Miami Indians in 1826. A hotheaded man, he engaged in long, rancorous public altercations with his political opponents during his second term. After his terms as governor he practiced law in Indianapolis with little success.

Ray was tall and wore his hair long and tied in a queue. A man described as "striking" and "egotistical," he was eccentric in his later years. No matter where he went, Ray always signed himself as "J. B. Ray, governor of Indiana and commander in chief of the army and navy."

* * * *

THE PORTRAIT of James Brown Ray brings the name of another painter into this discussion. The portrait has no signature, but Dunn is our authority for assigning it to Jacob Cox, dean of the Indianapolis artists during the post-Civil War period, and one of the most revered painters in the state.[30] The style or method of painting supports this attribution. Since the portrait is not dated, the circumstances of its execution are left in question. If James Ray sat for the portrait, it was made early in Cox's career as a painter, for Governor Ray died in 1848. If it was made at the order of Governor Baker in 1869, Cox would have used either a photograph or another painting.

A study of the portrait leads us to the conclusion that it was painted from life and not from a photograph or painting as in the case of previously mentioned works. Also, in comparing it with other portraits by Cox, it seems to be among the artist's earliest known portraits, dating before 1840,[31] and is therefore one of the earliest works in the collection. If the portrait is so early a production, it was not, in all probability, commissioned by the state. We may surmise that Ray conceded to the artist's wish to make a study of him, and that the painting remained in the artist's studio until Governor Baker acquired it in 1869. Although the execution is far from skillful, the artist has invested the figure with character and vitality—the strongest argument for the conclusion that the picture was painted from life. Ray's expression is not genial—he seems to have adopted here the sullen and cantankerous manner of his later years.[32]

Jacob Cox was born near Philadelphia in 1810, and his youth was spent in Philadelphia and in Washington, Pennsylvania. When he was about twenty years old, he went by boat, with his bride and his brother, from Pittsburgh to Cincinnati. In 1833, they came to Indianapolis, where the brothers established a stove, tinware, and coppersmith business. Jacob had displayed some talent for art in his boyhood days, but he was persuaded to take up a more practical trade and was discouraged from taking instruction in drawing and painting. The tinware establishment was very successful here, but Jacob found his eagerness to paint overshadowing his interest in business, and spare moments given to sketching and reading art books multiplied until painting became the dominant interest of his life. He opened a studio in Indianapolis in 1835 and began his long career as an Indiana painter, which was interrupted by a short stay in Cincinnati in 1842. His reputation grew rapidly, and within a few years he became the leading artist of Indianapolis, receiving many important commissions and attracting to his studio

---

[30] Dunn, *Greater Indianapolis*, I, 481.

[31] Peat assigns this portrait to the year 1840 and that of the following, Noah Noble (see below) to 1837 based on comparisons with other dated or datable portraits by Cox. In the light of recent conservation of these paintings, this editor believes that no such accurate dating can be assigned to the portraits particularly since both pictures are products of the artist's early career when his style was likely to be inconsistent. Until more conclusive documentary evidence can be found, the general dates of 1835, the date of Cox's earliest portraits, to 1840, have been given to these pictures.

[32] Ray's closely cropped hairstyle as depicted in the portrait before its 1978 conservation treatment did not conform to the account of the governor's appearance described above. There was evidence, however, to indicate that Ray was painted by Cox with long hair hanging straight down the back of his neck. Early photographs of the portrait confirmed this supposition. Damages to the canvas indicate vigorous overcleaning by a previous restorer in the area at the back of Ray's neck. The localized damage indicates either a purposeful change in the portrait to alter the sitter's appearance, or a misunderstanding on the part of the restorer as to the artist's intention. During the 1978 conservation treatment, the overpaint in this area was removed to reveal the dark shadow behind Ray's neck which still reads convincingly as long, straight hair.

7
JAMES BROWN RAY, 1835–1840
Jacob Cox, American*, 1810–1892
oil on canvas, 36⅛ x 29⅛ (91.7 x 74.0)
Unsigned

most of the art students of the period. He retained
his popularity until his death in 1892.[33]

[33] For more detailed information on Jacob Cox, see Wilbur D. Peat, *Paintings by Jacob Cox—A Retrospective Exhibition of Work by an Early Indianapolis Artist*, (ex. cat.) Indianapolis, John Herron Art Museum, November 8–30, 1941.

Noah Noble, 1794–1844
Governor December 7, 1831–December 6, 1837

NOAH NOBLE was born in Virginia and moved to Brookville, Indiana, in 1811 to join his brother James, a prominent lawyer and later United States senator. Largely self-taught, his business ventures in Brookville included land speculation and the operation of wool carding machines. He was commissioned a lieutenant colonel in the 7th Regiment, Indiana militia, in 1817 and a colonel in 1820.

Noble's political career began in 1820 when he was elected sheriff of Franklin County. He was elected to the Indiana House of Representatives in 1824 and was appointed receiver of public moneys for the Indianapolis land office in 1825. As a Whig, Noble was elected to the governorship in 1831 and was re-elected in 1834. It was during Noble's administration that a state bank was created and an internal improvements program was begun. Noble, who longed to succeed his brother in the Senate, was a candidate in 1836 and 1838 but was defeated in both elections. He continued in public office, however, as a member of the State Board of Internal Improvement from 1839 to 1841 and as a fund commissioner from 1841 until 1842.

Noble and his wife were well known for their lavish hospitality, entertaining public figures frequently. Oliver H. Smith, his opponent in the senatorial race, described Noble as "tall and slim, his constitution delicate, his smile winning, his voice feeble, the squeeze of his hand irresistible."

* * * *

THE PORTRAIT of Noah Noble is another of Jacob Cox's studio and raises the same queries regarding date and derivation as does the portrait of Ray. Like the Ray portrait, the portrait of Noah Noble was painted early in the artist's career, before 1840.[34] The paintings are strikingly similar in the pose of the subject, the facial expression and the self-conscious, inflexible method of rendering. Although lacking his technical ability at this point in his career, Cox infused the portraits with enough variety to reflect the very different personalities of the sitters. Noah Noble was a handsome, prepossessing man, and Cox has invested his portrait with refinement and grace. The use of clear, pastel tints and detailed attention to delicate background effects such as the quill pen, vine-like foliage, and gold tablecloth trim are befitting the governor's urbane manner.

Like the portrait of Ray, this painting probably remained in the possession of the artist until it was acquired by the state in 1869.

---

[34] See Note 31 above.

NOAH NOBLE, 1835–1840
Jacob Cox, American*, 1810–1892
oil on canvas, 36 x 29 (91.5 x 73.7)
Unsigned

David Wallace, 1799–1859
Governor December 6, 1837–December 9, 1840

DAVID WALLACE, born in Pennsylvania, moved with his family to Ohio where he attended school. He later moved to Brookville, Indiana, where he studied law and was admitted to the bar. He attended the U. S. Military Academy at West Point, graduating in 1821 as a second lieutenant. He served in the 7th Regiment, Indiana militia, with ranks of lieutenant, captain, and colonel.

Wallace served in the Indiana House of Representatives from 1828 to 1831, when he was elected lieutenant governor on the Whig ticket with Noah Noble. He was re-elected in 1834 and served until February, 1837, when he became a candidate for governor. In that election he defeated John Dumont, also a Whig. Wallace's administration was plagued with economic disaster as a result of the collapse of the internal improvements program. He was elected to Congress in 1841 but was unsuccessful in his bid for re-election in 1843. He was the Whig state chairman in 1846, a member of the constitutional convention in 1850, and was elected judge of the court of common pleas in 1856.

A dignified man with a judicious manner, he was also described as "a lover of books, and was one of the most delightful of readers." He is, however, most famous as the father of Lew Wallace.

****

THE PORTRAIT of David Wallace is the third in the collection by Jacob Cox and is unquestionably the best of the artist's early production. The subject has been seen and drawn more broadly, and the portrait is convincing in its suggestion of character. Cox successfully employs decorative devices to lend interest, rank, and dignity to the portrait. Used frequently throughout the early days of the Republic and well into the nineteenth century, the billowing deep maroon curtain, usually drawn back to reveal a pier or column, and the cloth covered writing table laden with books and documents are motifs seen in various arrangements. Holding his place in a book to give the viewer his attention, Wallace presents an expression that is incisive and resolute, and he impresses one as a man of convictions.

The success with which the artist has given these impressions leaves little doubt in one's mind that the portrait was painted from life. But in addition to these internal evidences, we have a statement from an eye-witness of the sittings. Lew Wallace, in his chatty story about his early aspirations to become an artist, tells how he found his father posing one day in Jacob Cox's studio: "When I heard that Mr. Cox painted pictures in oil, I nerved myself and boldly invaded his studio.

He was painting my father's portrait when I went in. The coincidence excused me. We became good friends, and not a few of my truancies were spent watching him at work".[35]

The context of this incident in the story of Lew Wallace's adventures suggests that the portrait was painted while his father was governor, between 1837 and 1840. An article in the *Indianapolis Journal* of September, 1841, supports the assignment of this general date.[36] Praising the "Elegant Gallery of Pictures and Portraits" by Mr. Cox in his studio, the article cites "the number and excellence of his portraits of our distinguished citizens," including Governor Wallace and Governor Bigger. Comparing the portrait with Cox's earlier portraits of Ray and Noble, a date of about 1840 is more accurate.[37]

While no other documentation has been found regarding this portrait, it can be assumed that, since the portrait was exhibited in Cox's own gallery, Wallace sat for his portrait at the artist's request.

It was probably acquired by the state from the artist in 1869.

---

[35] Lew Wallace, An *Autobiography*, New York and London, 1906 I, 49.

[36] "The Fine Arts in Indianapolis," Indianapolis *Indiana Journal* September 10, 1841, p. 1.

[37] Mary Q. Burnet, in *Art and Artists of Indiana*, New York, 1921, 80, implies that the portrait was painted between 1840 and 1842, an Louis E. Gibson in an article in the *Indianapolis News*, July 20, 1893, 5, col. 1, speaks of the portrait as having been made after Cox's retur from Cincinnati, which would place it around 1843. Based on th portrait's comparative artistic merit, Peat was in agreement with th later date of 1843. At the time, he was unaware of the 1841 newspap article cited in note 36, which conclusively establishes the earlier da of 1840.

9
DAVID WALLACE, c. 1840
Jacob Cox, American*, 1810–1892
oil on canvas, 36¼ x 29 (92.1 x 73.7)
Signed l.l. on book: J COX/IX . ? .

Samuel Bigger, 1802–1846
Governor December 9, 1840–December 6, 1843

SAMUEL BIGGER was born in Ohio, the son of a prominent Ohio legislator, and attended Ohio University, where he received both the A.B. and A.M. degrees, and then studied law. He moved to Indiana in 1829, eventually settling in Rushville.

Bigger served in the Indiana House of Representatives from 1833 to 1835, as circuit court judge from 1835 to 1840, and in 1840 was nominated for governor on the Whig ticket, defeating his Democratic opponent, General Tilghman A. Howard. As a result of the breakdown of the internal improvements program, Bigger's administration was plagued with the state's debts. He was nominated for re-election in 1843 but was defeated by James Whitcomb. He moved to Fort Wayne, where he resumed his law practice, and died suddenly two years later, while still a young man.

Although Bigger was not considered a brilliant man, his judgment was sound and he was popular. One contemporary commented that Bigger "had Lincoln's fondness for a joke without much of his skill in telling one." A large, dark-complexioned man, he was an enthusiastic and capable bass singer and violinist.

* * * *

THE PORTRAIT of Samuel Bigger is the fourth painting by Jacob Cox in the Governors Portrait Collection. In the previously mentioned *Indianapolis Journal* article of September, 1841, the portrait of Governor Bigger receives special praise, being described as "precisely what it should be, a perfect likeness." Since Bigger is most likely portrayed as governor (note the book marked "State Papers" on the shelf behind him), the painting can be assigned to the year 1841, just after Bigger assumed office. Although there are no records relating to its passing into the possession of the State, we may surmise that Governor Baker acquired the portrait from Cox in 1869.

The comment made by the writer of the *Journal* article indicates his attraction to the portrait's straightforward, unadorned manner. The stock decorative devices frequently used by Cox have been discarded, but the bookcase and writing table, laden with official papers and documents, lends the required gubernatorial air to the portrait without a staged effect. Patches of direct color relieve the sobriety of the plain grey background. Seated erect, an envelope in hand, Bigger is presented as a practical, serious man. There is a suggestion of nervous energy in his pose, conveying the strain that the governor is under as he tries to guide the destinies of a state almost bankrupt.

0
AMUEL BIGGER, 1841
acob Cox, American*, 1810–1892
il on canvas, 36 x 29 (91.4 x 73.7)
Unsigned

James Whitcomb, 1795–1852
Governor December 6, 1843–December 26, 1848

JAMES WHITCOMB was born in Vermont, moved to Kentucky, and graduated from Transylvania University. He studied law and was admitted to the bar in Fayette County, Kentucky, in 1822, before finally settling in Bloomington, Indiana, in 1824.

Whitcomb served in the Indiana Senate from 1830 to 1836, when President Jackson appointed him commissioner of the General Land Office, a position which he held until 1841. Whitcomb was elected governor on the Democratic ticket in 1843, defeating the incumbent governor, Samuel Bigger. Three years later he was re-elected. It was during Whitcomb's administration that the Indiana Hospital for the Insane, the Indiana Asylum for the Education of the Deaf and Dumb, and the Indiana Institute for the Education of the Blind were established. Whitcomb resigned as governor in December, 1848, upon his election to the United States Senate, where he served until his death on October 4, 1852.

Whitcomb was accounted a brilliant man by his peers. Although he was known for parsimony, he was also elegant of manner and dress and accumulated a fine library, which he left to DePauw University. One author remembers that Whitcomb was "as economical of time as of money, always reading when not engaged with business. It was not unusual to meet him in the street, absorbed in the contents of a book." He married quite late in life and left a five-year-old daughter an orphan upon his death.

* * * *

THE OFFICIAL portrait of James Whitcomb is the work of the Scottish artist, James Forbes. This and Forbes's previous commissions from the state were carried out in Evansville early in the fall of 1869. Like his portraits of Jennings and Boon, the portrait of Whitcomb was painted from another picture.

Whitcomb had died in 1852 and Governor Baker had some difficulty securing good pictures for Forbes to copy. The first that he found was an oil portrait made from a daguerreotype about 1849 when Whitcomb was in the United States Senate. The owner, Mrs. Claude Matthews of Clinton, Indiana, daughter of James Whitcomb, prized it highly and regarded it as an excellent likeness. The artist, on the contrary, did not find it a good model for his work, judging by his letter to Governor Baker: "After I had cleaned and varnished the portrait of Gov. Whitcomb, it looked so much improved, that I commenced a copy of it . . . I hope however you will find a daguerreotype or photograph of some sort for me to copy from—for tho this may be a *very cognizable likeness* It wants

individuality—or mental character.—Has a vapid expression that makes one feel they are looking on a poorly *painted* picture, instead of on the man himself."[38]

A damaged and faded daguerreotype was owned by a descendant in Chillicothe, Ohio, but due to its condition steps were not immediately taken to secure it, a photograph of it being borrowed instead. The *pentimento* in the portrait made visible by the fading of upper layers of pigment indicates a probable change in the position of the figure's head. Forbes must have felt the necessity to begin the portrait anew, once the photograph was in his hands. Judging from correspondence, the finishing touches were not added until the daguerreotype was in the artist's studio.[39]

When the portrait was finally finished, Forbes placed it on view in Evansville for the inspection of Whitcomb's old friends. "Drs. Bray, Casselberry, and De Bruler, Major Robinson and several others called to see Gov. Whitcomb's portrait, wrote Forbes to Governor Baker. "I am glad to say they each thought the likeness good tho some at first could barely recollect the features after so many years."[40] Like the other portraits by James Forbes, the study of Whitcomb, although largely from a photograph, has a good deal of pictorial charm and breadth of execution. The governor's dark suit and mass of black hair are placed against a warm gray background with a red tablecloth adding a pleasing note of color to the arrangement. The turn of the governor's head and gesture of his hand give the pose considerable animation. However, Forbes has failed to convey the intellectual force and fine character which are synonymous with Whitcomb's name. The rather listless eye and weak mouth are probably due to the poor prototypes Forbes had to follow, and, judging by remarks he made in his letters to Conrad Baker, he himself was not entirely satisfied with the result.

[38] Forbes to Governor Baker, September 27, 1869. Governor Baker's correspondence.

[39] Forbes to Governor Baker, September 27 and October 20, 1869; Claude Matthews to Governor Baker, September 27 and October 3, 1869; Forbes to John M. Commons, October 11, 18, 1869; R. R. Seymour to Governor Baker, October 20, 1869, Governor Baker correspondence. The daguerreotype was the property of R. R. Seymour of Chillicothe, Ohio, a brother-in-law of Governor Whitcomb.

[40] Forbes to Governor Baker, October 20, 1869. *Ibid.*

11
JAMES WHITCOMB, 1869
James Forbes, American, b. Scotland, c. 1800–?
oil on canvas, 36⅛ x 29⅛ (91.8 x 74.0)
Signed bottom center: Jas. Forbes Pinx

Paris Chipman Dunning, 1806–1884
Governor December 26, 1848–December 5, 1849

PARIS DUNNING was born in North Carolina and moved to Bloomington, Indiana, in 1823. He attended the academy at Greensboro, North Carolina, studied medicine in Kentucky, and finally studied law with James Whitcomb in Bloomington.

Dunning served in the Indiana House of Representatives from 1833 to 1836 and in the Indiana Senate from 1836 to 1840. In 1846 Dunning was elected lieutenant governor on the Democratic ticket, and became governor in December, 1848, when Whitcomb was elected to the United States Senate. Dunning, a Douglas Democrat, was again elected to the state senate in 1863 and was chosen to be president of that body. He then returned to Bloomington and his law practice, where he achieved success as a leading criminal lawyer.

Dunning was the only person in Indiana history who held all the offices of governor, lieutenant governor, state senator, president pro tempore of the state senate, and state representative. A contemporary described him as speaking "fluently and with marked emphasis. His style, both in speaking and writing, is nervous and bold."

* * * *

THE LIKENESS of Paris C. Dunning was the first state portrait painted by James Forbes from life. The artist's three earlier commissions—the portraits of Jonathan Jennings, Ratliff Boon, and James Whitcomb—had been done from other pictures, and judging from his correspondence with Conrad Baker, Forbes was aware of the superiority of portraits made from life and was looking forward to the opportunity of painting one or two of the former governors who were still living.

Governor Baker submitted to Dunning his plan of assembling the governors' likenesses, and Dunning consented to have his own painted at the earliest date possible. His reply to Baker was: "I will accommodate myself to Mr Forbes convenience, whom I will meet in Evansville on next Wednesday or Thursday, if that time will suit him .... Your recommendation of Mr Forbes is entirely satisfactory to me."[41]

The sittings began in September, 1869, and the picture was ready for delivery in about two weeks, both men having enjoyed the experience of watching the portrait take shape. "The Gov. seems much pleased to give me every advantage he can in the way of sitting," wrote Forbes. "He says 'he is here for the sole purpose and desires the portrait may be a success.'—It is of course unsafe to say any thing about it as yet but, I think Gov. Dunning has individual character enough to make the likeness as strong as I wish, if it should have no other merit—"[42]

The portrait reflects the confidence with which Forbes approached the project of painting his subject from life. The artist has been much more successful here in creating a pictorially "whole" effect—the body proportions are correct and the gesture is more fluid. The variety of textures and clarity of color lend a vivid tangibility. The "individual character" which Forbes admired so much in his model is well expressed. His friendly and candid eyes are fixed on the spectator; his posture is alert, and his expression reflects a genuine interest in people and events.

---

[41] Dunning to Governor Baker, September 17, 1869. Governor Baker's correspondence.

[42] Forbes to Governor Baker, September 27, 1869. *Ibid.*

CRIS CHIPMAN DUNNING, 1869
es Forbes, American, b. Scotland, c. 1800–?
on canvas, 36¼ x 29½ (92.1 x 75.0)
ned l.l.: Jas Forbes Pinx.

Joseph Albert Wright, 1810–1867
Governor December 5, 1849–January 12, 1857

JOSEPH WRIGHT was born in Pennsylvania, the son of a brick manufacturer, and moved as a boy to Bloomington, Indiana. His father died when Joseph was fourteen years old, and Wright worked his way through Indiana Seminary (later Indiana University) as janitor, bellringer, and occasional bricklayer. He was admitted to the bar in 1829 and opened a practice in Rockville.

Wright served in the Indiana House of Representatives (1833–1838), the Indiana Senate (1839–1842), and the United States Congress (1843–1845). In 1849 he was elected governor on the Democratic ticket, and in 1852 was re-elected under the state's new constitution for a term of four years. Wright's administration was highlighted by the adoption of a new state constitution and by the formation of a State Board of Education and a State Board of Agriculture. After his term as governor Wright served as minister to Prussia from 1857 to 1861. A firm supporter of the Union in the Civil War, he was appointed United States senator to the vacancy caused by the expulsion of Senator Jesse D. Bright, and served from February, 1862, until January, 1863.

A zealous Methodist and Sunday school supporter, Wright was "tall and raw-boned . . . and an effective speaker, mainly on account of his earnestness and simplicity." He composed Indiana's contribution to the words on the Washington Monument in Washington, D.C.: "Indiana knows no East, no West, no North, no South, nothing but the Union."

* * * *

JOSEPH WRIGHT's portrait in the collection is another by Jacob Cox. It was acquired for the state in Governor Baker's time, but since there are no records of the date or of the circumstances of its execution, or of its history prior to its placement in the State House, we can only speculate about its origin.

Since Wright did not return to Indiana after 1857 when he left to serve as minister to Prussia, it is likely that Cox painted the portrait before Wright left Indianapolis. The painting probably dates from late in Wright's second term of office since he appears in the portrait to be a man approaching fifty. The execution is such as to lead one to believe that the portrait was made from life: his set jaw and compressed lips imply an unyielding disposition; and the gesture of his hand toward a statute book clearly suggests his regard for the authority of the law.

The composition and coloring have been successfully arranged. The tones are deep and rich. A rosy glow pervades the background, creating a warm atmosphere and a convincing effect of depth. The well-modeled head is strongly illuminated, giving the face a ruddy hue and making it stand out clearly from the background.

It is interesting to note that Cox had painted five Indiana governors before the formation of the collection in 1869. In fact, the four previously mentioned portraits may have been displayed in the committee room of the State House at an exhibition of Cox's work, late in 1841.[43] One cannot help but wonder if the existence of this nucleus was not a large factor in encouraging Conrad Baker to initiate the project.

---

[43] Peat, *Paintings by Jacob Cox,* unpaginated.

13
JOSEPH ALBERT WRIGHT, before 1857
Jacob Cox, American*, 1810–1892
Oil on canvas, 36³/₁₆ x 29⅛ (92.0 x 74.0)
Unsigned

Ashbel Parsons Willard, 1820–1860
Governor January 12, 1857–October 4, 1860

ASHBEL WILLARD was born in New York, educated at Hamilton College, and then studied law. He moved to Michigan, to Texas, and then settled in Kentucky. Willard, a Democrat, spoke in New Albany, Indiana, while campaigning for James Polk in the 1844 presidential campaign, and the citizens were so impressed with him that they asked him to settle there. He moved to New Albany in 1845 and practiced law. He served in the Indiana House of Representatives (1850–1851), and in 1852 was elected lieutenant governor on the Democratic ticket with Joseph Wright. Willard was only thirty-six years old when he defeated Oliver P. Morton in the 1856 election for governor. Willard's administration was plagued with problems with the legislature, and he was forced to borrow money to pay the interest on the state's debt. A heavy drinker with longstanding health problems, in 1860 Willard, in a vain effort to regain his health, went to Minnesota where he died in October. He was the first of Indiana's chief executives to die in office.

Handsome, red-haired, blue-eyed, Willard was indisputably a charismatic figure and a man of tremendous charm and force. His abilities as a campaigner were extraordinary, his oratorical powers pre-eminent. In 1854 the *Western Democratic Review* described him as "the best popular orator in the United States."

* * * *

THE PORTRAIT of Ashbel P. Willard is the work of George W. Morrison, a fellow citizen of Willard in New Albany. Morrison was the leading portrait painter of the town and its vicinity, and was highly respected as a person and as an artist. He was born in Maryland in 1820, but spent most of his life in New Albany, dying there in 1893.[44]

Governor Baker's introduction to him came through Colonel Benjamin F. Scribner of New Albany, who called the governor's attention to a portrait of Ashbel P. Willard which Morrison had painted in 1857, three years before Willard's death. Scribner wrote: "This picture is still in Mr Morrisons possession, and is considered a *fine likeness* by *all* who knew Willard in his *best* days It [is] a half length with hands 29 x 36 price one hundred & fifty dolls without the frame."[45] It was sent to the governor for inspection in January, 1870, and as there was some delay in purchasing it, the New Albany press published some crusading editorials on the artist's behalf. The portrait was eventually acquired by the state and placed in the collection, much to the pleasure of the artist and his New Albany friends.[46]

Like most of Morrison's work, the technique is rather painstaking and tight; the pose is rigid, and the delineation of features is accurate but lacking in strong characterization. Morrison had a way of investing his subject with a mild, genial spirit, and the impression created by his study of Governor Willard is that of a calm, placid personality. Willard stands upright, facing his audience as though ready to address them, and holds a letter and a book in his hands. Behind him is a tan wall with an architectural column at the left. An arc-shaped shadow at the top of the canvas suggests that an arched frame, popular in the nineteenth century, was intended. Against the background, Willard's dark suit stands out in a positive way. This is one of Morrison's best portraits on record, and it adds materially to the collection of pictures in the State House.

---

[44] See Peat, *Pioneer Painters of Indiana*, for more detailed biographical information on Morrison, pp. 45, 52–53, 181, 235.

[45] Scribner to Governor Baker, August 3, 1869. Governor Baker' correspondence.

[46] George W. Morrison to Governor Baker, January 7, 1870. *Ibid.*

4
ASHBEL PARSONS WILLARD, 1857
George W. Morrison, American*, 1820–1893
Oil on canvas, 36¼ x 29⅛ (92.1 x 74.0)
Signed l.l. at base of column: G. W. Morrison Pinxt

Abram Adams Hammond, 1814–1874
Governor October 4, 1860–January 14, 1861

ABRAM HAMMOND was born in Vermont and came to Brookville, Indiana, when he was six years old. After attending the common schools he studied law and practiced in Greenfield and Columbus. A restless man all his life, he moved to Cincinnati in 1847 and practiced there until 1849, and, again after a few years in Indiana, in 1852 Hammond set out for San Francisco and practiced law with a prominent firm for three years. He later moved back to Indianapolis where he served as judge of the court of common pleas for Marion County. Well known as a capable lawyer, in 1856 Hammond, a former Whig, was elected lieutenant governor on the Democratic ticket with Ashbel Willard. When Willard died in office in October, 1860, Hammond served out the remaining three months of Willard's term as governor.

Medium-sized and compactly built, Hammond had a poker face and a self-contained manner. Contemporary observers wondered how he managed to build a law practice, since he was "not content to sit in his office and wait for a client." Soon after his term was over Hammond was severely afflicted with rheumatism and asthma, and he died in Denver, Colorado, in 1874.

* * * *

THE PORTRAIT of Abram A. Hammond was the second commission given by Governor Baker to John B. Hill, the young Indianapolis artist. It was made from life, eight years after the close of Governor Hammond's incumbency, and while he was practicing law in Indianapolis.

The sitter is portrayed very objectively, and the paint is applied in an indecisive, laborious way, with considerable emphasis on details of costume and lines of the face. Hill was not a skillful technician, and lacking experience as a portrait painter, he had a tendency to exaggerate minor elements, such as wrinkles, folds, and buttons. The color, too, is dull.

As one of the few extant paintings by Hill, and unquestionably his most important made from life, the portrait of Hammond is of more than passing interest. The tired and rather wan look on the governor's face was doubtless due to his poor health at the time the portrait was painted.

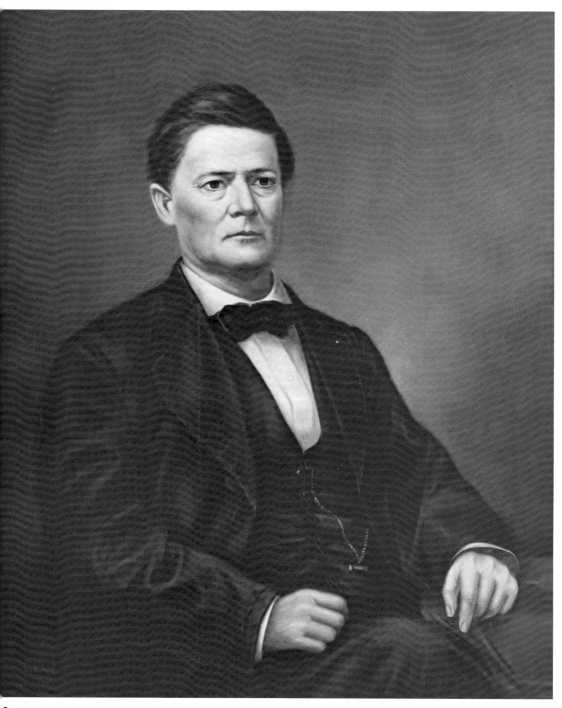

5
ABRAM ADAMS HAMMOND, 1869
John Bayless Hill, American*, 1849–1874
Oil on canvas, 36 x 29 (91.4 x 73.7)
Signed and dated l.l.: Jno. B. Hill./Pinxt/1869

Henry Smith Lane, 1811–1881
Governor January 14–16, 1861

HENRY LANE, who served the briefest term as governor (two days), was born in Kentucky where he was educated by private tutors and studied law. In 1835 he moved to Crawfordsville. He served in the Indiana House of Representatives from 1837 to 1838, and in the United States Congress from 1840 to 1843. Lane was active in the formation of the Republican party and in 1860 was elected governor. Both Lane and Morton had been active candidates for the nomination. Morton, who had been the nominee in 1856, had strong backing, but it was felt that Lane would better insure the support of conservative old-line Whigs. A compromise was worked out between the two whereby if Lane and Morton were elected and if the Republicans gained control of the new legislature, Lane would be elected to the United States Senate and Morton would succeed to the governorship. Thus, Lane was sworn in as governor on January 14, 1861, and two days later resigned the governorship upon his election to the United States Senate. He served as senator until 1867 as a strong advocate of union ideas and then returned home to private life in Crawfordsville.

One biographer wrote: "His public speeches glowed and scintillated with gems of original wit and fitly chosen anecdote." Another pointed out gently that Lane "was not a logical speaker, and as a debater he was excelled by many of far less reputation as an orator than he."

* * * *

THE PORTRAIT of Henry S. Lane in the State House was painted eight years after the governor's very brief occupancy of the executive chair. It is the work of Jacob Cox. Governor Baker sent word to Lane at his home in Crawfordsville about the collection of governors' portraits and suggested that Cox make his portrait. Lane answered: "I have received your letter of the 12th Inst. in reference to Painting my portrait, in pursuance of a provision of the last Legislature & I am much pleased with your selection of Mr. Cox as the artist. I will send a large Photograph by Brady which is thought to be a good likeness, ('painfully like the Original') I will give a sitting or two either at this place or Indianapolis as may best suit his convenience at any time which he may designate."[47] It is likely that Lane came to Indianapolis and gave Cox the necessary sittings in his studio.

The portrait represents the venerable governor and senator comfortably seated in a large red chair, holding a cane in his left hand. He looks out of the frame with deep-set, intelligent eyes, the white hair and beard contrasting with the dark shadows of the background. His pose is lifelike and his attitude amiable and gracious.

This study of Lane is the sixth and last portrait by Jacob Cox in the State House collection. It is the only one of his works made specifically for the collection.

---

[47] Lane to Governor Baker, August 16, 1869. Governor Baker correspondence.

6
HENRY SMITH LANE, 1869
Jacob Cox, American*, 1810–1892
Oil on canvas, 36⅛ x 29¹/₁₆ (91.8 x 73.8)
Signed and dated l.l.: J Cox/1869

Oliver Perry Morton, 1823–1877
Governor January 16, 1861–January 23, 1867

OLIVER P. MORTON was the first Indiana-born man to hold the office of governor. Born in Salisbury, Wayne County, Indiana, Morton worked as a hatter's apprentice for four years before he attended Miami University in Ohio and studied law both in Centerville, Indiana, and in law school at Cincinnati.

Originally a Democrat, Morton was one of the organizers of the Republican party, and in 1856 he ran unsuccessfully for governor against Ashbel Willard. In 1860 he was elected lieutenant governor on the ticket with Henry S. Lane and became governor in 1861 when Lane was elected to the United States Senate. Morton was re-elected in 1864 and served until 1867 when he was elected to the United States Senate, where he was a leading Radical Republican until his death in 1877. Morton served as governor during the critical period of the Civil War, and, although his terms were marked by conflict between the governor and the legislature, historian James Ford Rhodes called him, "The ablest and most energetic of the war governors of the Western States."

A forceful and passionate partisan of unquestioned intellectual and executive ability, Morton was a highly controversial figure throughout his political career. He was partially paralyzed by a stroke in 1865 and thereafter was obliged to walk with canes.

* * * *

THE PORTRAIT of Indiana's Civil War governor, Oliver Perry Morton, was painted by James Forbes. Correspondence between Governor Baker and the artist informs us that Baker had selected Forbes to paint Morton some time before the artist's visit to Indianapolis in the fall of 1869. Forbes looked forward to the undertaking with interest, and not without some anxiety, as is shown in his letter of October 20, 1869:

> I would beg to say—that However anxious I may be to paint the portrait of a gentleman of such eminent abilities as Gov. Morton, I am not sanguine he will, from any thing in the two portraits sent, select me to do it—and am unwilling he shall conclude I cannot do a better portrait than either with even less pains than I have bestowed on them.[48]

The two portraits referred to were those he had painted in Evansville of Governors Whitcomb and Dunning. Evidently both Morton and Baker were satisfied with the performances, for Forbes was given the honor of painting the Morton portrait. The sittings were probably in Indianapolis.

Forbes has succeeded in making a convincing likeness, and the boldness of the design is appropriate to Morton's determined, forceful disposition. Strong contrasts of dark hair and beard against light flesh tints and white shirt front, the sharp eyes and clear demarcation of the head against the background help to give the composition a striking effect. The impression is weakened, however, by the self-conscious artificiality of the gesture of declamation, and the governor's fixed expression, totally unrelated to the gesture.

Another portrait of Morton in the collection, done by T. C. Steele, belongs to the paintings of "epochal" governors ordered in 1916 for the executive office, and pays tribute to his leadership through the Civil War period. Since the pose is not the same as in the Forbes portrait, we know that Steele went to another source for his model; according to the local press the picture he used came from a relative of the war governor, "who declared the print an excellent likeness."[49] Steele's version of Morton is more reserved in spirit and more restrained in tone and color than the Forbes work. The subject appears several years older, and he looks off to the left in a relaxed, thoughtful attitude.

---

48 Forbes to Governor Baker, October 20, 1869. Governor Baker correspondence.

49 *Indianapolis News*, May 20, 1916, p. 17, col. 1.

7
OLIVER PERRY MORTON, 1869
James Forbes, American, b. Scotland, c. 1800–?
Oil on canvas, 36⅛ x 29 (91.8 x 73.7)
Signed l.l.: Jas. Forbes/Pinxt

Conrad Baker, 1817–1885
Governor January 23, 1867–January 13, 1873

CONRAD BAKER was born in Pennsylvania, received his education at Pennsylvania College, and studied law in Gettysburg. Baker moved to Evansville, Indiana, in 1841, and served in the Indiana House of Representatives from 1845 to 1846. In 1856 he was defeated for lieutenant governor on the Republican ticket with Oliver P. Morton. During the war he served three years as a colonel, and in 1864 he was successful in his bid for lieutenant governor. He became governor in 1867 when Governor Morton was elected to the United States Senate, and Baker was elected to his own term as governor in 1868. Baker is responsible for initiating the project to collect portraits of all Indiana governors. After his administration he entered the prominent law firm of Hendricks, Hord, and Hendricks, replacing Thomas A. Hendricks, his successor as governor.

The election of 1868 was marked by the absence of any declarations of misconduct or accusations against Baker. As one writer notes: "His administration had been characterized as an upright, honest and conscientious one, so much so that his honorable opponent found nothing to attack but the measures of the party of which Governor Baker was the chosen representative." Baker was heavyset, with sandy hair and whiskers and florid complexion.

* * * *

CONRAD BAKER had his own portrait painted late in 1869 or early in 1870, as he was completing the collection for the state. His respect for James Forbes had grown so steadily as work on the different paintings progressed that he selected the visiting Scotsman rather than one of the resident artists to make it. This was the sixth and last of the Forbes commissions.

Baker is shown sitting in a chair, his body turned toward the left, holding a letter in his hand as though discussing its contents. He is a handsome man with regular features, a heavy beard, and thin brown hair; his expression is genial and his attitude sympathetic. The same rich tones are used here as in Forbes's earlier compositions. Against a gray-green background the healthy ruddiness of Baker's face makes a strong color note; the whites of the shirt, collar, cuffs, and paper are set in strong opposition to the black suit; and touches of green on the back of the chair repeat the general tone of the background.

For about ten years the picture by Forbes was not in the collection. It was removed in 1933, at the request of Governor Baker's children, some of whom felt that it was not as good a likeness of their father as an oil painting done by Cox from life in 1883.[50] A more casual, intimate rendering, the painting includes only the head and shoulders in an oval format. Miss Clara Barrett-Strait, a New York artist known to the Baker family, was engaged to copy the Cox portrait for the State House. The Barrett-Strait portrait was removed from the collection in December, 1943, when the Forbes portrait of Governor Baker was reinstated.[51]

[50] The portrait of Conrad Baker by Jacob Cox is in the collection of the Indiana Historical Society, Gift of Mrs. J. L. Kirby-Smith, 1971

[51] The portrait by Miss Barrett-Strait was in the possession of Mrs. Evans Woollen, Sr., Indianapolis, in 1944, but can no longer be located.

18
CONRAD BAKER, 1869 (late) or 1870 (early)
James Forbes, American, b. Scotland, c. 1800–?
oil on canvas, 36 x 29 (91.5 x 73.7)
Signed l.l.: Jas Forbes

Thomas Andrews Hendricks, 1819–1885
Governor January 13, 1873–January 8, 1877

THOMAS HENDRICKS, nephew of former Governor William Hendricks, was born near Zanesville, Ohio, and moved with his family to Madison, Indiana, when he was a child. He was educated at Hanover College, graduating in 1841, and studied law in Chambersburg, Pennsylvania. Returning to Madison, the young Democratic lawyer soon moved into political life; he served in the Indiana House of Representatives, the constitutional convention of 1850, and in Congress. From 1855 to 1859 he was commissioner of the General Land Office in Washington, and he made a national reputation as one of the leading northern Democrats in the Senate during the Civil War and Reconstruction. After two earlier unsuccessful campaigns for governor, he was finally elected in 1873, the first Democratic governor elected in a northern state after the war. He was elected Vice-President of the United States in 1884 and died in office, less than nine months after his inauguration.

Hendricks was a popular politician and a good debater. His amiable manner led his opponents to complain that he had "not enough sincerity to be irritated by opposition." His political contribution was an essentially conservative one, attempting to fend off and hold back the revolutionary measures of the war and reconstruction periods.

* * * *

GOVERNOR THOMAS A. HENDRICKS had his portrait painted by an artist named Willian R. Freeman soon after he assumed office in 1873. Freeman, the fifth Indiana painter to be employed on the project, was well known in this region. He traveled rather extensively in connection with his portrait work, visiting Indianapolis more than once as he shuttled back and forth through Indiana and the neighboring states. Dunn reports that Freeman was "a transient here in 1873-4, who stopped at the Bates House and painted several portraits of citizens."[52]

Freeman was born in New York State about 1820 and came to Vincennes, Indiana, in 1849. He rented a studio there and painted portraits of members of some of the early families. Later he moved to Terre Haute, and at one time he lived in Madison. Following his short stay in Indianapolis, he went to San Francisco, and so far as is known, did not return to Indiana. He died in St. Louis about 1906.[53]

Freeman's canvas is one of the best in the State House collection. Hendricks sits upright in his office chair, looking off to the observer's right with a thoughtful expression. He appears relaxed; his hand, holding an Indianapolis newspaper, has dropped to his lap. His head is well drawn; the figure is fully modeled and features are clearly indicated. The artist has suggested a candid, honest, and amiable personality. Freeman's style is mellower than that of the painters we have discussed up to this point, and his colors, though limited to grays and reds, are pleasing and harmonious.

Thomas A. Hendricks, because of his achievements as a peace governor, was one of the four men chosen by Governor Ralston at the time of the state's centennial, for representation as an "epochal" governor. Steele's portrait made for this group seems to have been painted from a photograph taken late in Hendricks's life. According to the Indianapolis press, Governor Ralston was especially pleased with the study of "gentle, yet courageous Hendricks whom he, as a young man beginning his study of law, had as a friend. Members of the Hendricks family who have seen the portrait of their illustrious ancestor have expressed their admiration for the Steele painting."[54]

---

[52] Dunn, *Greater Indianapolis*, I, 481.

[53] See Peat, *Pioneer Painters of Indiana*, pp. 24–25, 41–42, 188–190 for more detailed biographical information on Freeman.

[54] *Indianapolis Star*, March 18, 1916, p. 7. The paintings of the four epochal governors are reproduced here.

19
THOMAS ANDREWS HENDRICKS, 1873
William R. Freeman, American*, c. 1820–c. 1906
oil on canvas, 36⅛ x 29 (91.7 x 73.7)
Signed l.r.: W. R. Freeman

James Douglas Williams, 1808–1880
Governor January 8, 1877–November 20, 1880

JAMES WILLIAMS moved to Knox County, Indiana, from Ohio as a child. He was educated in the common schools, and he farmed all his life. His nickname "Blue Jeans" reflected his customary apparel in suits of that material. The oldest of six children, at age twenty he took over the care of his brothers and sisters when his father died.

Williams's political career as a Democrat began as justice of the peace in Knox County and continued with many terms in the Indiana legislature in both houses in the thirty-one years between 1843 and 1874. He was elected to Congress in 1874 and to the governorship in 1876, defeating Benjamin Harrison by five thousand votes in the latter race. The extensive railroad strike of 1877 created problems for Williams, who sympathized with the strikers. He was an especially capable legislative leader and was identified with many important state laws.

"Blue Jeans" Williams was a large, rugged, rough-hewn man, six feet four inches tall, with a lot of black hair. Conrad Baker described him as "a man of strong, generous, emotional nature." He died in office in 1880.

* * * *

THE PORTRAIT of James D. Williams has puzzled historians for some time due to a lack of information regarding the artist who painted it. Dunn reported that it was painted by "a Mr. Colcord, an unknown transient."[56] Information from various sources has been accumulated since the first inquiries were made, but the story of Colcord's life and work remains sketchy. The earliest reference to this artist indicates that he was in Indianapolis in 1877, when he exhibited two portraits at Lieber's Art Emporium.[57] According to city directories of the period, an artist named Harry M. Colcord had a studio at 37 West Washington Street in Indianapolis in 1878 and 1879. An "H. Colcord" appeared as the contributor of a portrait in a catalogue for the 1878 exhibition sponsored by the Indiana Art Association, held in Indianapolis. The dropping of Colcord's name from the city directory after 1879 suggests that he left Indianapolis in 1880. It is then safe to assume that the portrait of James D. Williams was painted while the governor was in office, between 1877 and 1880.[58]

Colcord's manner of painting is characteristic of painters who have had little or no academic training, although the portrait reflects the artist's natural ability and sense of pleasing design. The flattened, angular forms create a severe effect, appropriate for the delineation of so plain and unaffected a man as James Williams.

Colcord's canvas is large, and upon it he has worked out an imposing composition. The governor sits facing the front, his right arm leaning on a table, his legs crossed, and his eyes directed toward the observer. The painting is laden with the cliches of official portraiture: a deliberate pose, table piled high with papers and books, and the ubiquitous column with draped curtain. Williams's customary "blue jeans" dress is a striking contrast to the strictly official setting. This portrayal of him as a tall, rawboned man with high cheekbones and large hands, is in keeping with early descriptions.

---

[55] Birth and death dates for Harry M. Colcord were found in the documentary files for the paintings by this artist in the Chicago Historical Society. The place of birth and death and the source for this information were not indicated, and they should therefore be confirmed before they are taken as fact.

[56] Dunn, *Greater Indianapolis*, I, 481.

[57] Indianapolis *Saturday Herald*, May 12, 1877, as cited in Peat *Pioneer Painters of Indiana*, p. 200.

[58] It is not known where Colcord went upon leaving Indianapolis, but a group of four dated portraits by a Henry (a name interchangeable with "Harry") M. Colcord in the collection of the Chicago Historical Society sheds a somewhat dim light on the subsequent activities of this evasive artist. Sometime between 1880 and 1885, presumably in Chicago, Colcord painted a copy of George Peter Alexander Healy's portrait of the Chicago merchant, banker, and philanthropist Walter Loomis Newberry, the original of which is in the Newberry Library in Chicago. A portrait painted from life by Colcord in 1892 of Reverend Henry Gideon Perry, a Chicago Episcopalian priest, provides confirmation of the artist's activity in Chicago, although as much as twelve years later. The Chicago city directories for 1891, 1892, and 1893 list a James Colcord, artist, at 169 North Clark Street, and given the knowledge of Henry Colcord's presence in Chicago at that time, it is tempting to assume a familial connection between them. In 1896, Henry Colcord is himself listed in the city directory as artist, at 1807 Auditorium Tower. In this year Colcord painted the portrait of Abraham Lincoln from an ambrotype in the collection of the Chicago Historical Society. The fourth dated portrait in the collection by Colcord is that of John Nelson Jewett, an Illinois state senator and prosperous Chicago lawyer. Painted in 1897, the portrait is the latest document of Colcord's artistic activity. More detailed information will hopefully be compiled at a future date regarding this artist whose reputation in his own time was sufficiently secure to attract several prestigious commissions.

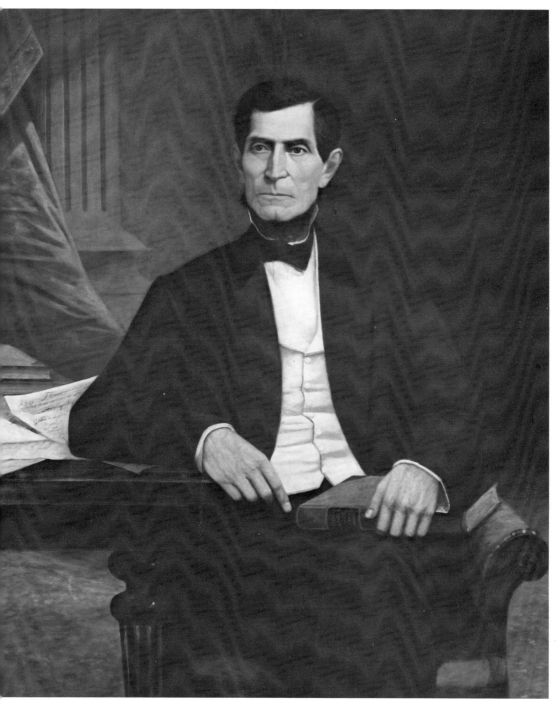

0
AMES DOUGLAS WILLIAMS, 1878–1879
Henry M. Colcord, American, 1828(?)–1906(?)[55]
il on canvas, 50 x 40 (127.0 x 101.1)
Unsigned

Isaac Pusey Gray, 1825–1895
Governor November 20, 1880–January 10, 1881
January 12, 1885–January 14, 1889

ISAAC GRAY was born in Pennsylvania in 1828 into a poor Quaker family. He was educated in common schools and settled in Union County, Indiana, as a dry goods merchant when he was twenty-seven years old. He served as a colonel in several regiments in the Union army during the Civil War and was a Republican candidate for Congress in 1866, losing the nomination to George W. Julian.

Gray was a state senator (1868–1870), then shifted parties—first to the Liberal Republican, then to the Democratic—and was elected lieutenant governor as a Democrat in 1876, serving a few months of Governor Williams's term when the governor died in office. Gray was elected governor in his own right in 1884. Forceful and ambitious, Gray was a willing candidate for either the Democratic presidential or vice-presidential nomination in 1892, losing the first to Cleveland and the second to Adlai Stevenson. He was appointed minister to Mexico in 1893.

Historian Jacob P. Dunn reports that Gray played an important role in Indiana's ratification of the Fifteenth Amendment to the Constitution. According to Dunn, as Republican president pro tempore of the state senate in May, 1869, Gray simply locked the door of the senate chambers and declared that a quorum was present for the vote, over the protests of Democratic members who insisted that they had already resigned their offices to prevent a quorum. This act by Gray as a Republican, Dunn suggests, essentially denied him the vice-presidency as a Democrat in 1892.

* * * *

WITH THE PORTRAIT of Isaac Pusey Gray there begins a series of five paintings of governors by T. C. Steele.[59] These are not to be confused with the four paintings made by him in connection with the state centennial in 1916.

Theodore Clement Steele, perhaps one of the most revered of all painters who remained in this state, was a native of Indiana. He was born in Owen County in 1847. When he was four years old, his family moved to Waveland, where he received his early schooling and some instruction in art at the Waveland Academy. He had very little formal training in painting, but he probably derived some help from visits to Cincinnati and Chicago in his impressionable years. His first activities as a professional painter took him to Battle Creek, Michigan, in 1870. Three years later he moved to Indianapolis and opened a studio on the Bradshaw Block, where he remained until 1880.

Portrait painting continued to be his chief activity during that period, and although he painted several prominent people, he was not commissioned to portray the governors then in office. In 1880, he went abroad for more intensive training at the Royal Academy of Art in Munich and stayed there five years.

Isaac P. Gray is portrayed in a gracious and sympathetic way by T. C. Steele. He is seated at ease in a large chair, upholstered in red leather, undoubtedly the one used in his executive office. This leads us to conclude that the portrait was painted in the State House.[60]

Governor Gray confronts the viewer with an astute look, his right shoulder turned toward the front. In his left hand he holds a book in which he marks a page, a device used commonly in portraiture with varying degrees of success, to indicate momentarily suspended activity and in this collection in the portraits of Ashbel Willard and David Wallace. The effect of light and air enveloping the model is unusually convincing; forms are well modeled without appearing hard, and the brush has moved across the canvas with apparent ease. The warm, olive background and deep red upholstery of the chair serve to complement the sallow complexion and sandy-colored hair. Steele seems to have reached his stride, so to speak, with this portrait, because technical problems have been solved with less effort than in the painting of Governor Albert Porter which preceded it.

---

[59] For a discussion of the governors' portraits painted by T. C. Steele in the context of a complete biography of the artist, see Selma N. Steele, Theodore L. Steele, and Wilbur D. Peat, *The House of the Singing Winds*, Indianapolis, 1966.

[60] This is supported by the recollections of the artist's son, Brand Steele, to Wilbur Peat. See Charles J. Oval, *Governors of Indiana*, Indianapolis, 1916, with supplementary notes about the portraits and artists added by Wilbur D. Peat, 1939, p. 95, in the Stout Reference Library, Indianapolis Museum of Art.

ISAAC PUSEY GRAY, 1888
Theodore Clement Steele, American*, 1847–1926
Oil on canvas, 40⅛ x 32⅛ (101.9 x 81.6)
Signed and dated u.r.: T. C. Steele/1888

Albert Gallatin Porter, 1824–1897
Governor January 10, 1881–January 12, 1885

ALBERT PORTER was born in Lawrenceburg, the son of a bank cashier and county recorder. He was educated at Hanover and Asbury colleges and studied law in Lawrenceburg. Originally a Democrat, he established himself in Indianapolis and quickly moved into political life as private secretary to Governor Whitcomb and reporter of the Indiana Supreme Court. In the storm over the expansion of slavery provoked by the Kansas-Nebraska Act of 1854, Porter joined the newly formed Republican party and was elected to Congress in 1858 and 1860 as a Republican.

Retiring from politics in 1862 he spent the next fourteen years building his personal fortune and establishing himself as an outstanding lawyer. He was appointed comptroller of the United States Treasury in 1877 and served until 1880. A suave and persuasive speaker, he overshadowed his opponent and was elected governor in 1880. Porter's administration was distinguished for public health measures, such as building state hospitals for the insane, establishing a state board of health, and draining large areas of marshland. President Benjamin Harrison appointed Porter minister to Italy, and he served in that office from 1889 to 1892.

After his term as governor, Porter collected materials for an extensive history of Indiana, but he died before he was able to complete the project. Porter was characterized by considerable energy and civic spirit. His name appears on almost every list of trustees for public projects in Indianapolis for many years.

＊＊＊＊

UPON HIS RETURN to Indianapolis in the summer of 1885 from Munich, T. C. Steele opened his studio again and began taking commissions for portraits. One of his first was that of Porter. Circumstantial evidence points to the probability that Porter postponed having his portrait painted until Steele returned, knowing something of the artist's ability and reputation. It must have been an important assignment for Steele, in that it would help greatly in re-establishing him in the city.[61]

Technically, the portrait reflects the academic method of painting that was prevalent in the Munich schools late in the nineteenth century. The palette is dark and limited, and the method of execution is controlled. A series of thin glazes are built up by the layering of brushstrokes, creating a luminosity and fine texture in the skin tones. In this early portrait, however, technique seems to have been an overriding concern, leaving the pose and expression somewhat frozen. While the portrait reflects the governor's kindly disposition, it displays none of the forcefulness of this accomplished man's character.

---

[61] The painting was exhibited at A. Lieber and Company, Indianapolis, on July 20, 1885; see, respectively, Steele, Steele, and Peat, *The House of the Singing Winds*, p. 33, and George Chambers Calvert, *Theodore C. Steele Memorial Exhibition*, Indianapolis, 1926, p. 17, no. 6.

LBERT GALLATIN PORTER, 1885
heodore Clement Steele, American*, 1847–1926
l on canvas, 40¼ x 30 (102 x 76.1)
gned and dated l.r.: T. C. Steele/1885

Alvin Peterson Hovey, 1821–1891
Governor January 14, 1889–November 23, 1891

ALVIN HOVEY was the son of impoverished Posey County pioneers who had come west to recover lost fortunes. Orphaned by the time he was fifteen years old, he received an education in the common schools and taught himself the law with books borrowed from a local lawyer. He began his legal career in Indiana by fighting to uphold the will of educational reformer William Maclure of New Harmony, bequeathing libraries for workingmen.

After serving in a company in the Mexican War that did not see action, Hovey was elected to the Indiana Constitutional Convention of 1850 and later as circuit court judge. He was Indiana Supreme Court judge for one year and United States district attorney for two. Hovey ran for Congress on the Republican ticket in 1858 and lost. He had a distinguished military career during the Civil War and was brevetted major general in 1864. After the war Hovey was appointed United States minister to Peru, where he served until 1870. He was elected to Congress in 1886 and governor in 1888. His administration was notable for the passage of election reform laws. He died in office, on November 23, 1891.

Indiana historian Jacob P. Dunn reported that some of Hovey's friends said that he believed himself to be Napoleon's reincarnation and honored the anniversary of Napoleon's death in solitary retreat. He was a distinguished-looking man with a military bearing.

* * * *

STEELE'S PORTRAIT of Alvin P. Hovey is an impressive canvas, large in size and bold in design.[62] It, too, may have been painted in the executive office. Dated 1889, it was painted in the year in which Hovey began his administration.

The governor is represented in a standing pose, almost full length, with his left arm and hand extended downward holding a book, and his right hand clasping a handkerchief. The right side of his face is shown as he looks toward an apparent source of daylight not visible in the picture. The strong, cool light falling on his face and down the side of his long coat emphasizes his stately, commanding figure. His firmly modeled features are set in earnest thought; and although he seems to be motionless, the artist has successfully suggested intensity of spirit and momentarily restrained activity. The colors are more subtly and successfully orchestrated than in the other portraits by Steele in the Governors Collection. Against an olive background the dark gray coat makes an effective area, especially as it assumes different values under the direct beam of light; and the warm tones of the face are echoed in the tan books and rose-colored cloth on the table at Hovey's left.

---

[62] The portrait of Hovey was also exhibited in the *Theodore Clement Steele Memorial Exhibition*, no. 59.

23
ALVIN PETERSON HOVEY, 1889
Theodore Clement Steele, American*, 1847–1926
oil on canvas, 50⅛ x 34 (127.3 x 86.4)
Signed and dated l.r.: T. C. Steele/1889

Ira Joy Chase, 1834–1895
Governor November 23, 1891–January 9, 1893

IRA CHASE was born in New York and educated at Milan Seminary in Ohio and Medina Academy in New York. Chase taught school and tried the hardware business before entering the ministry. He served one year in the Union army before being discharged for ill health. Chase entered the ministry and came to Indiana in 1867 as pastor in the Christian Church of Mishawaka, and he later served also at La Porte, Wabash, and Danville. His war service led to his appointment as Indiana G.A.R. chaplain in 1886 and his election as department commander in 1887.

Chase was elected lieutenant governor in 1888 and became governor upon Alvin Hovey's death in 1891. Chase was defeated when he ran for governor in his own right in 1892.

A campaign sketch in 1888 described Chase as "candid to the point of simplicity" and suggested that he was criticized by professional politicians as "wanting art." He continued his work as a minister during his term as lieutenant governor and governor.

* * * *

THE SITTINGS for the portrait of Ira J. Chase were given in 1892, probably at Steele's studio,[63] to which the artist moved shortly after his return from Munich. The Tinker home, Steele's studio, later became the site of the John Herron Art Institute.

In many ways, the Chase portrait is the best of the series painted by Steele for the official collection. Perhaps the better working conditions that prevailed in a well-equipped studio, away from the disturbances of executive routine, had much to do with its success. Another factor must have been the artist's mastery of a method which was most congenial to his temperament. The portrait has an airiness about it, reflecting the gradual drift in popularity away from the tight Munich academic style toward the new impressionist techniques. The broader execution and warmer palette create a convincing sense of atmosphere and depth, and a variety of textures are well expressed.

Governor Chase is seated erect in a mahogany chair, turning away from his desk toward the right. His attitude and personality are convincingly described by the artist, for he seems alert and attentive to whatever is going on around him. One is made to feel a fine character behind the eyes that look out from the canvas with an earnestness and understanding.

---

[63] Brandt Steele, son of the artist, related this information to Wilbur Peat. See Oval, *Governors of Indiana,* p. 103.

4
RA JOY CHASE, 1892
Theodore Clement Steele, American*, 1847–1926
il on canvas, 40¼ x 30 (102.2 x 76.2)
igned and dated l.r.: T. C. Steele/1892

Claude Matthews, 1845–1898
Governor January 9, 1893–January 11, 1897

CLAUDE MATTHEWS was born in Kentucky and graduated from Centre College in Danville in 1867. At age sixteen he had fallen in love with former Governor James Whitcomb's orphaned daughter, and he married her seven years later, after he graduated from college. They settled on a farm in Vermillion County, and he became successful as a farmer and especially as a stockbreeder. He was a founder of the National Association of Breeders of Short Horn Cattle in the United States and Canada in 1872.

Matthews, a Democrat, was elected to the state legislature in 1876 and ran unsuccessfully for the state senate in 1882. He served as Indiana secretary of state from 1891 to 1893 and was elected governor in 1892. Matthews, like William Jennings Bryan a free-silver supporter, was a favorite son candidate for the presidency in 1896.

As governor, Matthews was distinguished for his vigorous efforts against the White Caps, prizefighting, and horseracing. He was tall, powerfully built, and dignified. Contemporary observers described him as "a growing man" and pointed to his rapid progress in skill as a public speaker during his term as governor. He died of a stroke at age fifty-two.

* * * *

THE PORTRAIT of Claude Matthews is the fifth and last in the series by T. C. Steele from life. In coloration and use of direct studio lighting, it is very much like the portrait of Governor Gray. It was painted in the first year of Matthews's administration, and, like the portrait of Governor Gray, may have been painted in the State House.

There is nothing unusual about either the pose or the composition, and while the execution is most competent, it is without dash or eccentricity. Apparently, Claude Matthews did not present to the artist so rich a personality as did some of his predecessors, although he has the appearance of a capable administrator. Placed in an unadorned setting, his black suit silhouetted against a dark olive background, he sits rather stiffly in a mahogany chair, his hands and arms relaxed. The pose suggests a somewhat self-conscious subject only mildly interested in the experience of having his portrait painted.

Steele's portraits of the governors seemed to have attracted more comment than the paintings of other artists who had worked on the project. This was probably due to the growing interest in the official collection at the time and to the increasing popularity of the painter among his fellow townsmen. However, despite his success in this field, Steele gradually turned his attention to landscape painting and toward the end of his life produced very few portraits. The five by him in the State House are among his finest.

5
CLAUDE MATTHEWS, 1893
Theodore Clement Steele, American*, 1847–1926
Oil on canvas, 40 x 30 (101.7 x 76.4)
Signed and dated l.r.: T. C. Steele/1893

James Atwell Mount, 1843–1901
Governor January 11, 1897–January 14, 1901

JAMES MOUNT, the son of a Montgomery County farmer, was educated in the common schools. He served for three years in the Seventy-Second Indiana Infantry (1862–1865), with distinction for bravery in action, and attended the Presbyterian academy in Lebanon, Indiana, for one year after the war. Then, with his bride, he began farming as a tenant in his home county and succeeded well enough to purchase the land he farmed after ten years and owned five hundred acres by 1895. Especially interested in husbandry, he frequently lectured at farmers' institutes, where he established a political base for his later career.

Mount, the successful farmer, was sent by his neighbors to the state senate in 1888 and then ran, unsuccessfully, for Congress in 1890. After serving in 1892 as president of an important vigilante organization, the State Horse Thief Detective Association, he was elected governor in 1896 and served his full term. Mount was called upon to mobilize Indiana troops to serve in the Spanish-American War.

He was a small, wiry man, an entertaining speaker, and a prominent Presbyterian layman.

* * * *

THE PORTRAIT of James A. Mount is the work of James M. Dennis, a native of Dublin, Indiana, and a resident of Indianapolis during the sixties and seventies. Dennis was born in 1840. He studied in Cincinnati and lived in Indianapolis from 1865 to 1873 and again from 1875 to 1883. In the latter year he moved to Detroit, and continued to paint portraits, landscapes, and murals. He died on May 6, 1918.

Confirmation that Dennis painted the portrait of Governor Mount is found in a letter that he wrote to Jacob Dunn after he had moved to Detroit. After mentioning a period of study in New York, Dennis said: "I again returned to Indianapolis and painted many portraits and landscapes. Some of the portraits that were painted at that time were John C. New, for the Treasury Building, Washington, D.C.; Governor Mount, for the State House, Indianapolis; Jefferson Davis... and Joseph E. Johns[t]on... all from life."[64]

The second period of his sojourn in Indianapolis was from 1875 to 1883. It is puzzling to have him say that he painted Governor Mount's portrait for the State House at that time, because Mount was then living on his farm and had not entered political life. His election as governor was in 1896, thirteen years after Dennis had left the state.

Two alternatives present themselves. Either Dennis made the portrait approximately fifteen years before Mount became governor, or he returned to Indianapolis again in or around 1900 to paint it for the collection. His reference to the portrait as "for the State House" suggests the latter possibility. The date 1900 seems more plausible too, when the painting itself is analyzed. Mount appears as a man between fifty-five and sixty years of age, and not forty as he would have been in 1883. Dennis has used pastel instead of oil paints, a medium he used almost exclusively around 1900 and thereafter.

Another riddle that may be explained someday is why Dennis was not commissioned to paint any of the official portraits in the seventies when other local artists were being favored; yet, after leaving Indianapolis, he was called back (if the above conclusions are correct) to paint Governor Mount—and this at a time the city could boast of several capable and experienced painters to whom the governor could have turned.[65]

The portrait of James Mount is not very impressive as it hangs in the State House now, but due to its poor condition it is not a fair measure of the artist's work. At some time it was cleaned by somebody who did not know that it was a pastel and was unaware of the fraility of the medium, and much of the original color and drawing were removed.

---

[64] Dunn, *Greater Indianapolis*, I, 482.

[65] Unfortunately, no new information has come to light regarding the circumstances surrounding the commission of the Mount portrait. Scant biographical information on James M. Dennis is provided Arthur Hopkins Gibson, *Artists of Early Michigan*, Detroit, Wayne State University Press, 1975.

6
JAMES ATWELL MOUNT, c. 1900 (?)
James M. Dennis, American*, 1840–1918
Pastel on canvas, 45 x 34 (114.3 x 86.4)
Unsigned

Winfield Taylor Durbin, 1847–1928
Governor January 14, 1901–January 9, 1905

WINFIELD DURBIN was born at Lawrenceburg, Indiana, the son of a tanner. He attended the common schools of Washington County and, after serving in the Civil War, he enrolled in a commercial college at St. Louis. He spent ten years in Indianapolis working for a dry goods firm, then moved to Anderson, where he worked for his father-in-law as a banker and engaged in independent operations as a manufacturer. A dedicated party man, he was a member of the Republican state committee from 1890 to 1897, including four years as chairman of the executive committee.

Durbin was appointed colonel of the Indiana volunteer regiment in the Spanish-American War, and in 1900, after his return from Cuba, he was elected governor. As governor he took firm action against lynching and advocated both better highways and more state regulation of automobiles. He also ran for governor in 1912, but he lost to Samuel M. Ralston. He died a millionaire in 1928.

Durbin was enthusiastic about military appurtenances—uniforms, drill, etc.—and was a devoted Knight Templar and G.A.R. member.

* * * *

THE OFFICIAL portrait of Winfield T. Durbin is listed as the work of Seymour Thomas, New York artist, in Mary O. Burnet's roster of artists who painted the governors.[66] It is not known, however, whether a Durbin portrait was ever actually painted by Thomas.[67] The present portrait of Governor Durbin is the work of Wayman Adams and is one of six by this artist in the State House. The painting is not dated, but according to the local press it was completed and hung in 1920, fifteen years after Durbin's retirement from office.[68]

It is difficult to account for this lapse of time. Durbin did not want the legislature to pay for his portrait so he arranged with Wayman Adams to paint it with the intention of donating it to the state. The reports of the State Library, which frequently refer to the governors' portraits, speak of this gap in the collection between 1908 and 1916 and reiterate Durbin's promise to supply the missing item.

Durbin should have been very pleased with his portrait when it was finally hung. Adams has depicted him in a quiet, thoughtful mood, facing his audience squarely and holding on his lap a magazine or newspaper. Patches of stark white produce a crisp note, a harmonious balance to an otherwise dark palette. The pose is natural and the head well drawn. The paint is applied with facility yet with a

restraint and propriety befitting this subject. Durbin has the appearance of a successful businessman with a face that suggests a forceful personality.

The eminent portrait painter Wayman Adams was born in Muncie in 1883. Having copied the works of his father, a self-taught artist, Adams went on to study at evening classes at the John Herron Art Institute. In 1910 he went to Italy to study under William Merritt Chase, who was conducting classes in Florence, and in 1912 he went abroad again, accompanying Robert Henri to Spain. He had already opened a studio in Indianapolis, and upon his return from Europe he continued his work here as a portrait painter. A few years later he went to New York, where he achieved fame as a portrait painter and a teacher in his Elizabethtown, New York, school. He frequently returned to Indianapolis, where he received many commissions including the governors' portraits. Toward the end of his career he moved to his wife's native town, Austin, Texas, where he died in 1959.

[66] Burnet, Art and Artists of Indiana, p. 417.

[67] Although no record of a portrait by Stephen Seymour Thomas has ever been found, the artist was in Crawfordsville, Indiana, in 1904 paint the portrait of General Lew Wallace, now in the collection of the Indianapolis Museum of Art. At that time he may have made arrangements to paint a portrait of the governor, but this is, of course, speculation.

[68] Indianapolis News, May 18, 1920, p. 13, col. 1.

INFIELD TAYLOR DURBIN, 1920 (?)
ayman Adams, American*, 1883–1959
on canvas, 43⅛ x 36⅛ (109.5 x 91.7)
gned l.l.: Wayman Adams

James Frank Hanly, 1863–1920
Governor January 9, 1905–January 11, 1909

FRANK HANLY was born in Illinois in a log cabin, an accident of fortune from which he derived considerable political benefit in the course of his career. He was educated in Illinois common schools and at Eastern Illinois Normal School, Danville. Moving to Warren County, Indiana, in 1879, he taught school and worked as a common laborer until he was admitted to the bar in 1889. The next year he was elected to the state senate, and in 1894 he won a congressional seat. He moved to Lafayette in 1896, after failing to win renomination, and practiced law. After an unsuccessful try for the Republican nomination for United States senator in 1898, he was elected governor in 1904.

As governor, Hanly crusaded against liquor, horseracing, and political corruption, even going so far as to prosecute members of his own administration for embezzlement. An electrifying speaker, Hanly went on after his term as governor to organize a group of prohibition lecturers—more like revivalists than lecturers—called the Flying Squadron, and in 1916 he joined the Prohibition party and was its candidate for President of the United States. He died in an automobile accident in 1920.

* * * *

THE PORTRAIT of J. Frank Hanly is also by Wayman Adams, but it predates the one of Governor Durbin by seven years. It is the earliest of this artist's work in the State House, and in many respects his best. In addition to his signature and the date on the canvas, we have the following record of its execution in the Indiana State Library *Bulletin* of November, 1913: "The last Assembly appropriated funds for the portraits of J. Frank Hanly and Thomas R. Marshall. Wayman Adams has finished the portrait of Mr. Hanly and it now hangs in the State Library. Mr. Marshall's has not yet been painted." This was almost four years after Hanly's administration closed.

A product of an era whose artists emphasized technical virtuosity, Wayman Adams applied richly textured brushstrokes with directness and speed. In each of the six official portraits by Wayman Adams the artist has employed his masterful artistic technique to reflect the individual character of his subject. In the portrait of Governor Hanly, the heavy, loosely applied paint accentuates the sitter's rugged and brusque character. The colors are deep and earthy. Hanly's swarthy face and hands, his black suit and hair, and his white vest are seen against a ruddy brown background. The composition is severe in its simplicity; there is nothing to enrich the background, and no paraphernalia surrounds the model. With eye fixed intently on the viewer Hanly faces front wit his left hand gripping his thigh. The pose sugges an alert and forceful leader, while the facial ex pression is one of shrewd deliberation.

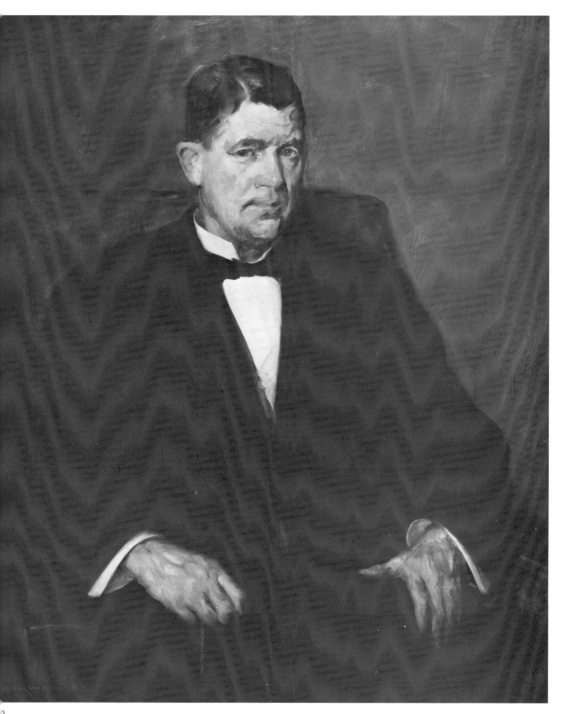

8
AMES FRANK HANLY, 1913
ayman Adams, American*, 1883–1959
l on canvas, 38 x 32 (96.5 x 81.3)
gned and dated l.l.: Wayman Adams/1913

Thomas Riley Marshall, 1854–1925
Governor January 11, 1909–January 13, 1913

THOMAS MARSHALL, best remembered for his eight years as Vice-President under Woodrow Wilson, was born in North Manchester, Indiana. His father was a physician. He graduated from Wabash College in 1873 and was admitted to the Columbia City bar soon after. Although he was a popular public speaker and active in local Democratic politics, Marshall was still only a small town lawyer when he received the nomination for governor in 1908, a compromise dark horse candidate.

Marshall was elected and was a popular governor, although his attempts to have the state adopt a new constitution failed. A few progressive measures, such as a child labor law and a corrupt practices act, were enacted under Marshall's leadership, but many more that he urged were defeated. During his terms as Vice-President he became well-known nationally for his wit, achieving fame for his remark, delivered as an aside during a Senate debate, "What this country needs is a really good five cent cigar."

Slight of stature and impeccably groomed, Marshall continued as a popular orator after retiring from the Vice-Presidency. His autobiography is an entertaining record of his career.

* * * *

THE PORTRAIT of Thomas R. Marshall, the third by Wayman Adams, was painted in Washington, nearly seven years after the end of Marshall's governship and toward the close of his second term as Vice-President of the United States. The sittings were held in his office during December, 1919, and a report of the work's completion came through the story of the Washington correspondent of the *Indianapolis News* that a "very lifelike portrait of Vice-President Marshall is on exhibition at his office here. It was painted by Wayman Adams, a New York artist, formerly of Indianapolis. An appropriation to pay for it was made by the Indiana legislature."[69]

The artist has shown Marshall in a seated pose, relaxed, but not without dignity. He appears to be turning toward his right, his hands hanging listlessly from the arms of a chair. One gets the impression that he was a sagacious gentleman, with considerable will power and inner force; and it is easy to understand, through the portrait, how his personality and industry brought him national prominence. Adams has recorded Marshall's likeness with so suave a technique and with such restraint of color that an air of distinction permeates the canvas.

---

[69] *Indianapolis News*, December 15, 1919, p. 12, col. 8; the portrait is illustrated in the *News*, December 20, 1919 on p. 17.

9
THOMAS RILEY MARSHALL, 1919
Wayman Adams, American*, 1883–1959
Oil on canvas, 43 x 36 (109.3 x 91.4)
Signed u.l.: Wayman Adams

Samuel Moffett Ralston, 1857–1925
Governor January 13, 1913–January 8, 1917

SAMUEL RALSTON was born in Ohio and moved to near Spencer, Indiana, in 1865, where his family farmed. After attending the common schools during winter months, Ralston attended normal schools in Valparaiso and Danville, and taught school for several years. Later he read law in Spencer, was admitted to the bar in 1886, and settled in Lebanon. An active Democrat, he ran for secretary of state in 1898 and lost. He also lost the gubernatorial nomination to Thomas R. Marshall in 1908, but in 1912 he was the Democratic nominee and was elected; he defeated Albert Beveridge, Progressive, and former governor Winfield Durbin, Republican. Among many other progressive measures enacted under his leadership, the state park system was initiated and a public service commission was created to regulate utilities. Ralston, who was Beveridge's personal friend and admirer, also defeated Beveridge for the Senate in 1922.

In 1924 the Democratic presidential nomination was virtually Ralston's for the accepting after a long, complex battle in the convention, but Ralston stunned the convention by withdrawing his name. His reason, though unexplained at the time, was his precarious health.

Ralston was a man of undisputed integrity and, according to contemporaries, "there was no bluster or pretense about him."

* * * *

SAMUEL M. RALSTON'S portrait was the second commission received by Wayman Adams from the state[70] and the first to be painted by him while the subject was in office. The sittings were held in the artist's Indianapolis studio in the State Savings and Trust Building on Market Street, and the portrait was completed in December, 1916.[71] A local newspaper reported,

> Mr. Adams is just finishing a portrait of Governor Ralston, and the work is going to stand out as one of the young artist's best. He has the Governor in a characteristic pose, and those who know the Governor intimately say Mr. Adams has done a distinctive piece of work.[72]

Ralston is shown in a front view pose, his right hand in his pocket and his left hand holding some papers. The gesture, exposing a wide expanse of vest and a dangling pocket watch, draws attention to the governor's portly figure. Technically, the picture is exceptional: the artist has worked rapidly and with apparent ease, and has caught the

likeness as the newspaper article suggests; he ha seen the head clearly and drawn it well, and he ha studied the character of the sitter sympathetically Adams has placed the sitter close to the picture plane, so that the viewer is made to feel Ralston' casual, direct nature.

---

[70] An article in the *Indianapolis News,* of March 14, 1916, state that Ralston agreed to sit for the portrait at Adams's request. While th circumstances surrounding the commission are unknown, it is likel that the portrait was painted expressly for the State House collectior

[71] While the canvas bears the date "January, 1916," contemporar newspaper articles indicate that the portrait was not completed until later date. Peat's date of December, 1916, is not documented, but h probably had this information from the artist.

[72] *Indianapolis News,* May 20, 1916, p. 17, col. 8.

30
SAMUEL MOFFETT RALSTON, 1916
Wayman Adams, American*, 1883–1959
oil on canvas, 43¼ x 36⅛ (109.9 x 91.8)
Signed and dated u.r.: Wayman Adams January/1916

James Putnam Goodrich, 1864–1940
Governor January 8, 1917–January 10, 1921

JAMES GOODRICH was born and raised in Winchester, Indiana. He attended public schools and the DePauw preparatory department in 1885. After his admission to the bar in 1887, Goodrich practiced law in his home town and quickly moved to prominence in Republican politics, serving as state chairman from 1901 to 1910 and national committeeman, 1912 to 1916. A highly successful businessman, he moved his practice to Indianapolis in 1910 and accumulated a large fortune in farmland, coal mines, grain elevators, and banks. He was elected governor in 1916 and served during the demanding years of World War I. Major achievements during his administration included planning a state highway system and creating the Department of Conservation.

In 1920 Goodrich was a favorite son candidate for the presidential nomination, losing to Warren G. Harding, who put him to work as special emissary to Russia. By 1922 Goodrich was considered one of America's best informed observers of Russian conditions. Goodrich also served on Hoover's American Relief Administration and commissions to plan for the St. Lawrence seaway. For many years he was an important figure at the Republican national conventions as the friend of presidents and the man behind the scenes in the Indiana delegation.

Goodrich devoted considerable attention and money to philanthropy in his last years, giving Wabash College more than a quarter of a million dollars in addition to smaller gifts to other schools.

* * * *

THE PORTRAIT of James P. Goodrich was painted while he was in office, but it did not enter the collection until more than twenty years later. Goodrich decided to have Wayman Adams paint it and forestalled an appropriation by the legislature by offering to present the portrait to the state himself.

Sittings were held in Indianapolis in December, 1920, but when the work was completed, the governor did not feel that the likeness was entirely satisfactory. After a lapse of time Adams made certain alterations according to Goodrich's suggestions, but still the portrait was not accepted. When other changes failed to satisfy Goodrich, the portrait was set aside with the thought that another might be painted.

No satisfactory portrait was made, however, during James Goodrich's life, and after his death in 1940, steps were taken to have the one by Adams hung in the State House. Pierre Goodrich, the governor's son, Colonel Richard Lieber, and other intimate friends of the late governor suggested certain modifications which the artist carried out to their satisfaction and the painting was accepted. Pierre Goodrich supplemented the legislature's appropriation to meet the artist's fee, and the portrait was placed in the State House in 1943.

The portrait's arrangement is striking in its effect of dark and light. Strong illumination on the face and collar is picked up again at the bottom of the picture by the rolled newspaper which the model is tightly gripping. The pose creates a strong vertical and horizontal pull, a forceful composition made severe by an unadorned background and a scarcity of accessories. The likeness is good, but, probably due to the several later changes, the portrait falls short of Adams's best work. The expression is set, and the deliberate pose and expression of strength and conviction appear rigid.

51
JAMES PUTNAM GOODRICH, 1920–1943
Wayman Adams, American*, 1883–1959
Oil on canvas, 43 x 35⅞ (109.0 x 91.2)
Signed u.l.: Wayman Adams

Warren Terry McCray, 1865–1938
Governor January 10, 1921–April 30, 1924

WARREN MCCRAY was born near Kentland, a banker's son, and was educated in the public schools. He clerked in his father's bank from the time he was fifteen years old and took over as president when his father died in 1913. McCray's financial interests also included a chain of grain elevators and a stock farm on which he bred Hereford cattle. McCray served as treasurer for the Northern Hospital for the Insane from 1904 to 1912 and was a member of the Indiana Board of Agriculture from 1912 to 1916. He also held appointive offices during World War I relating to agricultural planning.

McCray was elected governor in 1920. His personal financial affairs suffered severe reversals during his governorship, and he was forced to resign in 1924 after being convicted of mail fraud in a case relating to his financial collapse. McCray served three years in a federal prison, then returned to Kentland to rebuild his stock farm. He later received a full pardon from Herbert Hoover.

* * * *

WARREN T. MCCRAY'S portrait for the State House was painted by Robert W. Grafton, a prominent Indiana artist. The picture bears no date, but it is said to have been painted in 1927, three years after McCray submitted his resignation as governor. It is a rather frank portrayal of the man. He is shown in a chair, leaning forward with his right arm extended on a table, his right hand resting on a large sheet of paper, and his left hand pressing against his leg. Although the picture does not convey a strong personality, it seems to suggest forcefulness tinged with shrewdness.

The technique is realistic in the rendering of features and details; the drawing is tight; and, except for the flesh tints, the colors are cold and grey. Lacking breadth of execution and pleasing color organization, the portrait loses much of its pictorial effectiveness.

The artist, Robert Grafton, was born in Chicago in 1876. He received most of his instruction in art at the Art Institute there, then traveled and painted in England, France, and Holland. Upon his return to this country, he made his home in Michigan City, Indiana, and soon gained wide recognition for the variety and sentiment of his pictures. Although he painted figure compositions and murals, he is best known for his portraits of educators, professional men, and public officials. The three which he painted for the state—of McCray, Jackson, and Leslie—are among his most important commissions. He died in 1936.

ARREN TERRY McCRAY, 1927
bert W. Grafton, American*, 1876–1936
on canvas, 40 x 30 (101.5 x 76.2)
isigned

Emmett Forrest Branch, 1874–1932
Governor April 30, 1924–January 12, 1925

EMMETT BRANCH was a Martinsville native, the son of a rather droll couple, who named their other children Olive Branch, Leafy Branch, and Frank Oaks Branch. Emmett, the first Indiana University graduate to become governor, graduated in 1896 and went on to study law.

Branch served as an officer in the Spanish-American War and was elected to three terms in the Indiana House of Representatives, serving from 1903 to 1909. He served on the Mexican border from 1916 to 1917 and in World War I. A Republican, in 1920 he was elected lieutenant governor on the ticket with Warren T. McCray. When Governor McCray resigned, Branch succeeded him and completed that term.

Branch was essentially a small town lawyer and businessman, practicing law and running his father's grain company for most of his life in Martinsville. He was tall and thin with shaggy hair.

＊ ＊ ＊ ＊

THE PORTRAIT of Emmett Branch is the work of an Indianapolis painter, Simon P. Baus. It was painted in 1927, two years after Branch left office, and was accepted for the gallery of governors in 1928.[73] Branch was living in Martinsville at the time, but the sittings were held in Baus's studio in Indianapolis.

According to the artist, Branch enjoyed the experience. As the sittings drew to a close, he was frequently accompanied by Mrs. Branch who added much to the genial atmosphere of the studio. The governor's main concern had to do with his glasses: he could not decide at first whether to be painted with them on or to take them off. He finally left them on.

The portrait shows him in a front-view position, leaning slightly forward with his eyes directed toward the spectator through large, dark-rimmed glasses. His pose is natural and unassuming, while his expression is kind and attentive. His blue-black suit is seen against a tan background, and a striped necktie adds a colorful touch to the composition. A certain decorative charm has resulted from the artist's tendency to simplify forms and emphasize the pattern throughout the picture.

Simon Baus, the artist, was born in Indianapolis, and except for a few trips to the Southwest, he spent most of his life in his native city. He received his first instruction in drawing under Otto Stark at Manual Training High School, and later he entered an evening class conducted by William Forsyth. Upon the opening of the Indianapolis Art Association's school, Baus studied under J. Ottis Adams, continuing there as a part-time student until 1911. Baus painted many notable Indiana people during his career as an artist, which he supplemented financially by working in the Indianapolis Post Office as a postal clerk for forty-five years. In 1966, Baus moved to Kent, Ohio, where he died three years later.

---

[73] The portrait was reproduced in the *Indianapolis News*, January 1928, with mention that it had just been accepted for the gallery governors at the State House.

3
MMETT FORREST BRANCH, 1927
imon Paul Baus, American*, 1882–1969
il on canvas, 40 x 32 (101.7 x 81.3)
igned and dated l.l.: BAUS/27

Edward L. Jackson, 1873–1954
Governor January 12, 1925–January 14, 1929

ED JACKSON, the son of a millworker, was born and educated in Howard County, Indiana. He studied law and opened his practice in Kennard. In 1898 Jackson entered politics in New Castle and served as Henry County prosecuting attorney; four years later he was appointed circuit court judge. His term as secretary of state was interrupted by his army enlistment in World War I; after his discharge he returned to his political career at the State House.

In 1924 Jackson, a Republican, was elected governor. His administration was plagued with repercussions from political scandals involving D. C. Stephenson and the Ku Klux Klan, and during his term as governor Jackson himself was tried on charges of bribing Governor McCray but was acquitted under the statute of limitations. Following his term Jackson resumed his law practice, working in Indianapolis until 1937, and then moved to Orleans in southern Indiana to raise cattle and run an apple orchard. Jackson suffered a paralyzing stroke in 1948 and was bedfast until his death.

* * * *

THE PORTRAIT of Governor Ed Jackson was the second made for the state by Robert W. Grafton, painted midway in Jackson's administration in 1927. That it was made at Dunes State Park should be of general interest: Jackson was greatly impressed by the unique beauty of the Indiana dunes, and the consummation of the acquisition of the tract by the state for a park during his administration was a source of satisfaction to him. Since this enthusiasm was shared by the artist, we may believe that the portrait was created under most favorable circumstances.

Grafton has sympathetically interpreted his subject. Jackson is shown seated in a three-quarter pose, his head turning back toward the observer. His appearance as well as his personality seems faithfully described. Grafton's meticulous and prosaic method of working, together with his predilection for somber colors, has resulted in a dull effect. Not even the very pink complexion which he has given his model relieves its sobriety.

4
DWARD L. JACKSON, 1927
obert W. Grafton, American*, 1876–1936
on canvas, 40 x 30⅛ (101.6 x 76.5)
gned and dated l.r.: Robt W. Grafton/1927

Harry Guyer Leslie, 1878–1937
Governor January 14, 1929–January 9, 1933

HARRY LESLIE was born of pioneer parents in West Lafayette. While a student at Purdue University Leslie played football, miraculously surviving the tragic 1903 train wreck that killed sixteen of his fellow team members en route to Bloomington. After many operations to repair extensive injuries, he graduated from Purdue and received his law degree from Indiana University. Leslie opened his law office in Lafayette, became involved in Tippecanoe County politics, and was elected county treasurer in 1912 and 1914. He engaged in farming from 1914 to 1924, serving also as a bank president.

Leslie, a Republican, was a representative in the Indiana house for four years and its speaker in 1925 and 1927 before his election as governor in 1928. A blunt, simple man, Leslie had an unusual talent for friendships and as governor was known for his straightforward style of administration. His term as governor coincided with the beginning of the Great Depression, and among his efforts to ameliorate its effects a special legislative session was called in 1932 to reduce taxes and expenses of government.

Following his governorship Leslie became a founder, and eventually the president, of a life insurance company in Indianapolis. Down-to-earth and witty, Leslie boasted storytellers like George Ade and Will Rogers as good friends.

* * * *

THE THIRD PORTRAIT by Robert W. Grafton in the State House is that of Harry G. Leslie. It was painted in 1929, the governor's first year in office. A certain amount of spirit and animation have been suggested by the forced pose: Leslie leans forward, his left arm on a table and his right hand on his knee, regarding the observer with a look of shrewd scrutiny.

The technique, like that of other paintings by Grafton, is deliberate and painstaking; the colors are dark, while their monotony is only slightly relieved by a deep red necktie and rosy flesh tints. Shadows are heavy, and the transition of forms from shadow into light is startling. While the painting is lacking in pictorial quality, it unquestionably presents the sitter with exactitude.

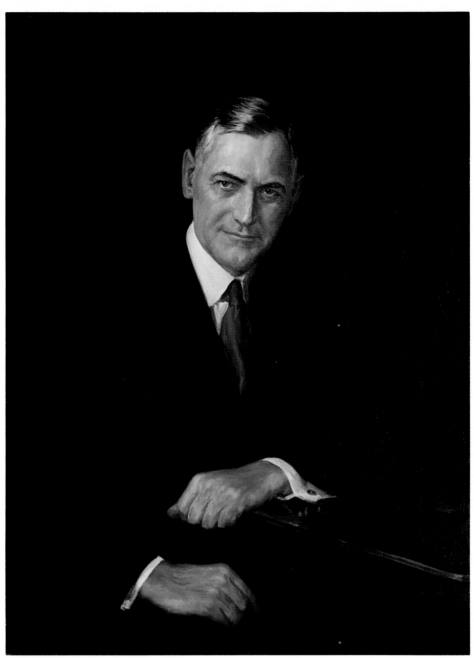

35
HARRY GUYER LESLIE, 1929
Robert W. Grafton, American*, 1876–1936
oil on canvas, 40 x 30¼ (101.6 x 76.8)
Signed and dated l.r.: Robt W. Grafton/1929

Paul Vories McNutt, 1891–1955
Governor January 9, 1933–January 11, 1937

PAUL MCNUTT was born in Franklin, Indiana, and was educated in the Martinsville public schools. After graduation from Indiana University in 1913 and Harvard University Law School in 1916, McNutt practiced law briefly with his father in Martinsville. He served as an officer in the army in World War I and returned in 1919 to teach at Indiana University Law School. He was appointed dean in 1925 and held the office until he was inaugurated as Indiana's governor in 1933, the first Democrat to hold that office since Samuel Ralston.

McNutt's political career was based initially upon his American Legion career: he was Indiana commander in 1927 and national commander in 1928–1929. Elected governor in 1932, McNutt took office two months before Franklin Roosevelt was sworn in as President, and the Indiana governor's program of emergency legislation anticipated the New Deal in many particulars. McNutt was a bold, strong leader (described as a "Hoosier Hitler" by his critics) and a highly effective governor. Centralizing the governor's administrative control, McNutt reorganized 169 state departments into 8 main departments (the measure was repealed in 1941), and he instituted the "2 percent club" among state patronage workers for the support of the Democratic state party.

McNutt served from 1937 to 1939 as High Commissioner to the Philippines, from 1939 to 1945 as administrator of the Federal Security Administration, from 1942 to 1945 as chairman of the War Manpower Commission, and from 1946 to 1947 as first United States ambassador to the Philippine Republic. McNutt then retired from public service to practice law in New York, Washington, D.C., and Manila. He also served as officer for several life insurance companies and in 1950 became chairman of the board of United Artists Corporation. The strikingly handsome McNutt was a capable administrator and a canny politician. He was also, however, obviously ambitious for the presidency during the Roosevelt era and therefore destined to be disappointed.

＊ ＊ ＊ ＊

PAUL MCNUTT was the sixth governor to select Wayman Adams to paint his portrait for the official collection. Although the artist was living in New York at the time, he came to Indianapolis at the governor's request to carry out the commission. This was in the summer of 1933. Sittings were held in one of the studios of the John Herron Art Institute, and rather than let the enterprise interfere with administrative duties, the governor had his secretary accompany him so that letter could be dictated while he posed.[74] Upon completion, the portrait did not satisfy McNutt and his friends, and a second one was undertaken. This time, the executive office at the State House became the studio. The work progressed as well as could be expected under the circumstances, and when the portrait was finished, it had the approval of the governor.

McNutt faces the front, sitting rather stiffly in chair, with his right elbow resting on a table. A letter held loosely in the fingers of his right hand draws the eye to the lower edge of the canvas, accentuating the long vertical axis of the composition. The canvas is large and more colorful than any of the earlier portraits by Adams. The characterization seems weak, but the decorative quality and facile brushwork appropriately express the governor's urbane, affable manner.

---

[74] *Indianapolis Star,* June 20, 1933, p. 9, col. 7; August 13, 193 rotogravure section, p. 1.

36
PAUL VORIES McNUTT, 1933
Wayman Adams, American*, 1883–1959
oil on canvas, 51⅞ x 40⅛ (131.8 x 101.9)
Signed u.r.: Wayman Adams

Maurice Clifford Townsend, 1884–1954
Governor January 11, 1937–January 13, 1941

CLIFFORD TOWNSEND was born on a farm and attended school in Blackford County, Indiana. After working as a teamster and in a factory, he graduated from Marion College, Grant County, taught in the common schools, and then served for fourteen years as school superintendent for different counties. He entered politics as a representative in the Indiana house and was elected lieutenant governor in 1932. Townsend's mother nominated him for governor at the 1936 Democratic state convention, and he was elected.

During World War II Townsend used his farm experience in government service, directing the Office of Agricultural War Relations, Agricultural Conservation and Adjustment Administration, and Food Production Administration. In 1943 he resigned from federal service and returned to Indiana to manage his farms in Blackford and Grant counties. Townsend was the Democratic candidate for the United States Senate in 1946 and was defeated by William E. Jenner.

An informal, folksy man, "Cliff" Townsend was credited with the safety measure of having all school buses painted yellow for instant identification.

* * * *

THE PORTRAIT of Governor M. Clifford Townsend was painted by Cornelius C. Zwaan, an artist who had come to Indianapolis in 1935. He had impressed Townsend and others with his ability to draw with exactness, and Townsend conceded to the artist's wish to paint his portrait. Zwaan made two paintings. The first was kept by Mr. and Mrs. Townsend, and a second was painted for the official collection in 1938. According to the *Indiana History Bulletin*, the portrait was accepted and hung in the State House in the spring of 1940.[75]

The picture represents the governor seated comfortably in a chair, his head turned so that he looks directly out of the canvas. Bookshelves and a desk in the left background give the composition an illusion of space. The smooth, linear style and rather literal choice of color is characteristic of much contemporary portraiture, possibly reflecting the popularity of large color photographs. The dominant mood of the portrait is one of geniality: Governor Townsend's pose is natural as he looks toward his audience with a calm, amiable expression.

Cornelius C. Zwaan, the artist, was born in Amsterdam in 1872 and attended the Ryks Academy there. He made several trips to the United States, painting portraits in different parts of the country. He lived in Milwaukee and a number of other cities before moving to Indianapolis in 1935. During his stay here, Zwaan painted many of Indianapolis's leading citizens. In 1940, he moved to Detroit, where he died in 196- In 1973 the Indianapolis Museum of Art held a retrospective of Zwaan's work in which the portrait of Maurice Clifford Townsend was a prominent feature.

[75] *Indiana History Bulletin*, XVII, no. 5, May, 1940, pp. 219–22

37
MAURICE CLIFFORD TOWNSEND, 1938
Cornelius Zwaan, Dutch, 1872–1964
oil on canvas, 44¼ x 36 (112.4 x 91.5)
Signed and dated l.r.: Cornelius Zwaan/1940

Henry Frederick Schricker, 1883–1966
Governor January 13, 1941–January 8, 1945

HENRY SCHRICKER was born in North Judson, the son of Bavarian immigrants, and attended Starke County public schools. He ran the *Starke County Democrat,* a weekly newspaper, for eleven years, then went into banking.

In 1924 Schricker, a Democrat, ran unsuccessfully for the state senate, but in 1932 he was elected to the same post. After serving as lieutenant governor from 1937 to 1941 he was elected governor in 1940 and again in 1948, becoming the first governor to be elected to two four-year terms. Challenged by Republican legislatures in both terms, Schricker's administrations were notable for the repeal in 1941 of the government reorganization laws of 1933 and legislative attempts to make welfare department records available to the public in violation of federal confidentiality requirements. Schricker was twice defeated for the United States Senate (in 1944 and 1952). Reportedly Franklin Roosevelt offered him the vice-presidential nomination in 1944, and Schricker declined. When his name came up as a possible candidate for the Presidency, he said with rare candor and modesty that the suggestion embarrassed him, since "a man ought to know his own limitations." He received national recognition in 1952 when he nominated Adlai Stevenson for President at the Democratic National Convention.

Schricker was a tremendously popular politician. He was described as a "typical Hoosier" and a small-town boy. An inveterate cigar smoker and tobacco chewer, Schricker excelled at the art of the political banquet and "the art of remembering people." He was spare, wore his pince-nez spectacles on a black ribbon, and with a sure sense for symbolism claimed a white hat as his political trademark.

Schricker was vice-president of an investment firm from 1944 to 1948; following his second term as governor he became president of an insurance company. He retired in 1960 to his home at Knox.

* * * *

THE FIRST PORTRAIT of Governor Henry F. Schricker was approved and accepted for the collection on April 27, 1943. It is the work of Marie Goth, the first woman commissioned by a governor to paint his official portrait.

Born in Indianapolis in 1887, Marie Goth attended Manual Training High School where she received sound instruction in drawing under Otto Stark. Later studies took her to New York where she attended the Art Students' League and painted under the best-known artists in the East. In 1923, she moved to Brown County, Indiana, and she became a charter member of the Brown County Art Gallery Association in 1926. Governor Schricker, James Whitcomb Riley, Paul V. McNutt, and General MacArthur were a few of her many prestigious sitters. She died in Brown County in 1975.

Governor Schricker sits erect in a Windsor chair, a favorite of Goth's in her Brown County studio where the sittings were held. She has portrayed Governor Schricker in a cordial mood, his eyes fixed on the observer with an interested, sympathetic look. A twinkle in his eye and the upward curve of his mouth suggest his droll humor. The governor's trim gray suit is seen against a deep maroon curtain, and his necktie repeats the color of the background. Goth's style is bold, combining skillful brushwork with a good knowledge of color and design.

38
HENRY FREDERICK SCHRICKER, before 1943
Marie Goth, American*, 1887–1975
oil on canvas, 42 x 36 (106.7 x 91.5)
Signed l.r.: MARIE Goth

Ralph F. Gates, 1893–1978
Governor January 8, 1945–January 10, 1949

RALPH GATES was born in Columbia City and continued to call it home throughout his life. After receiving both undergraduate and law degrees from the University of Michigan, Gates returned home to enter his father's law practice. He served in World War I and upon his return became politically active as his father had been. Eventually he served as Indiana commander of the American Legion and as Republican state chairman.

In 1944 Gates was elected governor, his first public office and the first Republican to be elected governor of Indiana since 1928. During his administration state departments were created to deal with problems of revenue, flood control, veterans' affairs, and traffic safety. A lively, dynamic man, who spoke effectively in a deep, gravelly voice, Gates's popularity was frequently attributed to his grass roots familiarity with the state.

Following his term as governor, Gates resumed his law practice in Columbia City, eventually being joined by both his son and his daughter, and continued to be active until 1974. He was for many years a force in state politics, acting as GOP national committeeman from 1947 to 1961. Much of his retirement was spent at his home on Crooked Lake, where the Ralph Gates Nature Preserve was dedicated in the spring of 1978.

* * * *

HOWARD PECKHAM facilitated the task of having a portrait painted of the modest and reluctant Ralph Gates. In 1945, Peckham consulted Wilbur Peat regarding the choice of an artist who, in accord with the governor's wishes, had not previously painted a portrait for the official collection.[76] The governor, absorbed in the affairs of the state, regarded having his portrait painted as an unpleasant duty. Pressure from outside sources concerning the selection of an artist made the subject even more loathsome to Gates. When Randolph Coats was chosen as the artist for the commission, Howard Peckham was obliged to make excuses for Gates, who apparently postponed the project in 1945. The portrait was painted in the summer of 1946,[77] with sittings held in the governor's office at the State House. To date no information regarding the commission has been found in the hand of Coats or Gates, although Mrs. Gates recalls that her husband had a favorable reaction to the portrait.[78]

Coats has posed the governor in a red upholstered chair with his right shoulder toward the viewer, holding a document or letter in his left hand. His relaxed yet erect position conveys a sense of dignity and determination. The essential features of the painting, the face and foreground details, are recorded by the artist in a meticulous linear manner which he reserved primarily for portrait work, while the background and subordinate details are by contrast more freely rendered. Coats's painting method involved the gradual buildup of clear tints of color, resulting in a translucency of skin tones for which the artist was frequently praised. Unfortunately, the pigment vehicle in this case has yellowed significantly with age, and some of the original delicacy and freshness have been lost.

The flamboyant, popular Randolph Coats was an accomplished painter and educator. Born in Richmond, Indiana, he attended the John Herron Art Institute and the Cincinnati Academy of Fine Arts, and studied independently in Europe. He returned to Indianapolis in 1922, maintaining a studio there until his death, but often summering at Cape Cod or the Smoky Mountains. Coats was a charter member and president of the Indiana Artists' Club, and he produced three films about art. Primarily known for his portraiture, most of Coats's commissions came from prestigious Hoosiers who knew and admired the artist's work. His involvement with the Governors Portrait Collection included the painting of two of the governors' portraits, Gates and Schricker, and an extensive restoration project on thirty-six of the portraits in 1953.[79]

---

[76] Howard Peckham to Governor Gates, April 27, 1945; Howard Peckham to Frances Norris Streit, April 15, 1946. See, File pertaining to Governors' Portraits, Indiana Historical Bureau.

[77] A photograph of Gates with the completed portrait was published in the *Indianapolis News,* August 29, 1946.

[78] Mrs. Phil McNagny, Jr., to the editor, September 23, 1978. Files pertaining to Governors' Portraits, Indiana Historical Bureau.

[79] "The Governors Take a Cleaning," *The Indianapolis Star Magazine,* September 20, 1953, p. 4, illus.

9
RALPH F. GATES, 1946
Randolph LaSalle Coats, American*, 1891–1957
Oil on canvas, 45⅛ x 34 (104.6 x 86.3)
Signed l.r.: RANDOLPH COATS—

Henry Frederick Schricker, 1883–1966
Governor January 10, 1949–January 12, 1953

A SECOND PORTRAIT of Schricker was commissioned in the governor's second term in 1952, this time from Randolph Coats, who had previously painted the portrait of Governor Gates. The portrait is smaller than the others in the official collection, and has the casual appearance of a wallet photograph. A light shining through the parted red drapery casts a bright beam on the governor's face, outlining the shape of the face and reflecting luminous skin tones. The literal use of color is in keeping with Coats's meticulous style and contributes to the photographic effect. The governor's kind, amiable personality is still conveyed, even through this degree of literalism.

)
ENRY FREDERICK SCHRICKER, 1952
andolph LaSalle Coats, American*, 1891–1957
l on canvas, 30 x 25 (76.2 x 63.7)
gned and dated l.r.: RANDOLPH COATS/1952

George N. Craig, b. 1909
Governor January 12, 1953–January 14, 1957

GEORGE CRAIG was born in Brazil, Indiana. He received his law degree from Indiana University and practiced with his father, a staunch "Jeffersonian" Democrat. During World War II he attained the rank of lieutenant colonel while serving in Europe, and after discharge he became involved in the American Legion on local and state levels, finally as national commander. He initiated the American Legion's "Tide for Toys" campaign, designed to distribute toys to foreign children.

Craig was elected governor on the Republican ticket in 1952. The Department of Corrections was created during Craig's administration, and the State Department of Health was reorganized to provide greater mental health care. He was featured on the cover of *Time* magazine in 1955— characterized as one of Eisenhower's favorite young Republicans, "a swift-footed, swashbuckling lawyer politician." However, Craig's political future was subdued when several of his close advisers were convicted in 1958 of bribery in acquiring state highway construction contracts.

Following his term as the "travelingest governor" in the state, Craig continued to travel, directing several business corporations and practicing law in Washington, D.C., and Los Angeles. In 1967 he returned to his quiet Brazil law practice and Owen County farm.

* * * *

BY VIRTUE of her artistic ability and with the aid of a persistent agent, her mother, Frances Norris Streit was chosen over fifty applicants to paint the official portrait of Governor Craig.

Streit received artistic training at John Herron Art Institute and at the State University of Iowa. During her course of study at Herron, she received several awards, including a bronze medal given by the Beaux Arts Institute of Architectural Design, for mural design. In 1943, Streit moved to New York, where she continued to paint portraits and teach art until 1973, when she retired to concentrate on mural design. She currently lives in Merrick, New York.

Before the work began, Streit had photographs of Governor Craig taken from several angles, and Mrs. Craig selected a pose that best reflected her husband's personality. Although photography is generally intended only as a convenience to reduce the number of sittings, in this case the artist was able to work from a photograph so that a one-hour sitting was all that was required of Craig to bring the portrait to completion. Before the work on the official portrait was begun, Streit painted a portrait of Mrs. Craig which the governor's wife

commissioned as an anniversary gift to her husband.

The composition of the Craig portrait is interesting and casual, although credit for its organization belongs primarily to the photographer rather than to the artist. Perched on the edge of his desk, Craig confronts the viewer with a relaxed expression. A repetition of rectangular shapes emphasizes the governor's robust, stocky appearance. Transverse diagonal movements lead the eye from the center of the composition to the flags flanking the figure: the Indiana and American Legion flags are additions to the composition which highlight Craig's political achievements.

Generally speaking, a portrait painted from a photograph rather than from life achieves verisimilitude but lacks a good deal of character. Highly idealized,[80] the Craig portrait is flattering but at the expense of both likeness and vitality. The two-dimensional linear scheme contributes a decorative quality to the painting, but the literal use of color lessens its appeal. The set expression and textureless quality of the work are among the many pitfalls of painting a portrait from a photograph rather than from life.

[80] Both the *Indianapolis Times* and the *Indianapolis News* covered the unveiling of the portrait in Craig's office on January 7, 1955. Craig commented that the portrait flattered him. A comparison of a contemporary portrait, that done for the *Time* magazine cover, confirms this opinion.

GEORGE N. CRAIG, 1954
Frances Norris Streit, American*, b. 1919
Oil on canvas, 44 x 36¼ (111.7 x 92.0)
Signed and dated l.r.: Frances Norris Streit 1954

Harold W. Handley, 1909–1972
Governor January 14, 1957–January 9, 1961

HAROLD HANDLEY was born in La Porte, Indiana, and graduated from Indiana University. He helped his father with the management of a furniture company in La Porte and became sales representative for a North Carolina-based furniture manufacturer.

Handley's political career in the state senate (1940–1941) was interrupted by his army service during World War II. Upon his return he was elected to the state senate in 1948 and lieutenant governor in 1952. Handley ran for governor and lost in 1952 but was elected governor in 1956. Handley raised some controversy when he ran for the United States Senate in 1958 midway in his term of office. He lost the Senate race to Democrat Vance Hartke and returned to the State House to complete his term. Handley was accessible to both the press and the public, establishing an unusual rapport with the citizens.

In 1961 Handley began an Indianapolis public relations and advertising firm convinced that, although a novice in the business, he would "go out and sell it." A large, gregarious man, Handley's political trademark was a blue polka-dot tie.

＊ ＊ ＊ ＊

PLANS TO commission a portrait of Governor Handley were underway by 1958, when Hubert Hawkins, then the Director of the Indiana Historical Bureau, sought the advice at the John Herron School of Art of Professor Garo Antreasian.[81] One of the artists mentioned by Antreasian, Donald Mattison, Dean of the art school, seemed a natural choice. Mattison was a close friend of Governor Handley, and the governor was reportedly pleased to have the tedium of sitting for his portrait relieved by hearty conversation.[82]

Four two-hour sittings were held in the summer of 1960 in Mattison's studio at the John Herron School of Art, and the artist completed the portrait with the aid of several photographs. Mattison's method of painting a portrait involved the use of mirrors through which he perceived his subject to achieve a once-removed, objective point of view. While the advantages of such a procedure are debatable, Mattison has not sacrificed immediacy and warmth for objectivity in the Handley portrait. A bold, forceful design emphasizes the vigor and enthusiasm which characterized Handley's administration.[83]

Lounging with legs crossed casually, Handley dangles his hand over the arm of a Windsor chair. The governor's attire, a blue suit and blue and white polka-dot tie, was his political trademark. Handley's crossed legs are thrust out of the picture

plane toward the viewer with an aggressive effect. The palette is limited to browns and modulated shades of blue, augmenting the severity of the composition.

Donald Mattison studied art under Eugene Savage at Yale and won the coveted Prix de Rome in 1928. Upon his return from Rome in 1931, Mattison taught at Columbia University, the New York School of Design and New York University. In 1933, Mattison became Dean of John Herron School of Art, a position he held until 1970. A skilled administrator, Mattison was a key figure in the expansion of the art school. As an accomplished portrait painter, he received many prestigious commissions. He died in 1975 in Indianapolis.

[81] Hubert Hawkins to Garo Antreasian, September 30, 195; Garo Antreasian to Hubert Hawkins, October 5, 1958. File related Governors' Portraits, Indiana Historical Bureau.

[82] Interview by the editor with Mrs. Harold Handley, Septembe 1977. Information concerning the circumstances of the commission was supplied by Mrs. Handley.

[83] An article in the *Indianapolis Times*, February 15, 1960, cove the unveiling of the portrait and Handley's comments. According the article, the governor "hoped future generations would view t portrait in reference to the accomplishments of his administratio rather than of him as an individual." The portrait was also reproduce in the *Indianapolis Star*, February 16, 1960.

AROLD W. HANDLEY, 1959
onald Mattison, American*, 1905–1975
on canvas, 46 x 40 (116.8 x 101.6)
gned and dated l.l.: DONALD M. MATTISON/1959

Matthew E. Welsh, b. 1912
Governor January 9, 1961–January 11, 1965

MATTHEW WELSH was born in Detroit, Michigan, and moved to Vincennes in 1924. His father was a securities broker active in Democratic politics. Welsh graduated from the University of Pennsylvania and from the University of Chicago Law School and returned to Vincennes to practice law. A Democrat, Welsh served in the Indiana House of Representatives, but his term ended when he resigned to join the navy in 1943. After the war he served as United States attorney and state senator before being elected governor in 1960. His term was marked by the enactment of a 2 percent sales tax to raise crucial revenues.

Welsh, a tall, slender, dignified man, once said he had two basic rules: "it never costs you to be a gentleman" and "you try to base everything on fact, so get all the facts." In 1965 Lyndon Johnson appointed Welsh to represent the United States as part-time chairman of the International Joint Commission on Waterways with Canada, designed to protect and maintain water levels along the United States-Canadian border. Later he resumed his law practice in Indianapolis, and he ran again for governor in 1972, losing to Otis R. Bowen.

* * * *

EDMUND BRUCKER was a natural choice as artist for the official portrait of Matthew E. Welsh. Brucker had already painted a picture of the new governor in 1960 for the cover of *Indiana Business and Industry Magazine.* [84] The popularity of this portrait resulted in an official commission for Brucker in 1964, the last year of Welsh's term. The sittings were given by Welsh in the artist's studio at the Herron School of Art. Brucker was impressed by Welsh's co-operative manner in posing, and the governor was delighted by the result.

Through careful studio lighting, Brucker has accented his subject's fine, elegant features, and has captured the expression of a confident, perceptive character. The governor stands at his desk, the downward thrust of his gesture creating a strong vertical axis, emphasizing his slender and dignified form. The color scheme, modulated tones of gray-green, is relieved by the warm spot of red in Welsh's tie. The stark patterning of the stationery in the governor's hand, with its prominent logo, draws undue attention in an otherwise textureless rendering.

Active as a portrait painter in Indianapolis since 1938, Edmund Brucker has recorded the likenesses of many prominent people around the state, including Dr. and Mrs. Norris Shreve, Mrs. Otis R. Bowen, and Colonel A. Weir Cook. In 1967, the artist retired from his post of almost thirty years as a professor at the Herron School of Art, and he currently lives in Indianapolis. Brucker represents a dwindling group of Indiana artists whose rigorous artistic training has prepared them for the highly skilled profession of portrait painter.

---

[84] See cover, *Indiana Business and Industry Magazine,* March, 19... The portrait was given to Governor and Mrs. Welsh by the Democratic party, and it now hangs in the Welsh home in Indianapolis.

43
MATTHEW E. WELSH, 1964
Edmund Brucker, American*, b. 1912
oil on canvas, 46⅛ x 36 (117.2 x 91.4)
Signed and dated l.r.: Edmund Brucker/1964

Roger D. Branigin, 1902–1975
Governor January 11, 1965–January 13, 1969

ROGER BRANIGIN was born in Franklin, Indiana, graduated from Franklin College, and received his law degree from Harvard University. He practiced law in Franklin, Louisville, and Lafayette before serving in World War II; after the war he returned to his law practice in Lafayette.

Following an unsuccessful run for the governorship in 1956, Branigin, a Democrat, was elected governor in 1964 by a record-breaking plurality. The poll tax and personal property tax on household goods were abolished during his administration, and the "right-to-work" law was repealed. He was a highly entertaining public speaker, storyteller, and wit, well known for his salty language. When asked to comment on his appeal to ordinary people, Branigin, the Harvard-educated lawyer, slyly replied, "People ask me if I'm for the common man. . . . I'm a Hoosier, a Baptist, and a Democrat, and, by God, you can't get much commoner than that."

Branigin ran as a favorite-son candidate for President in the Democratic primary in 1968, losing to Robert F. Kennedy, and returned to Lafayette to practice corporation law. He also served as a trustee of Franklin College and the Lilly Endowment and, in an appropriate expression of his interest in Indiana history, was a board member of the Indiana Historical Society.

* * * *

GOVERNOR BRANIGIN'S interest in cultural activities around the state naturally yielded many contacts in the arts. He wisely consulted the proprietor of an Indianapolis art gallery, Carl Lyman, regarding an artist to paint his official portrait. Lyman's suggestion, Helen B. Duckwall, was a fitting, though not an immediately obvious, choice.

Duckwall is well known for her portraits of children and women in pastel, which she executed on commission through Lyman Brothers, Inc., in the late 1930s. Born in Sheridan, Indiana, she attended John Herron School of Art and the Philadelphia School of Fine Arts. Most of her artistic career was spent in Indianapolis, but she currently lives in Clearwater, Florida.

The sittings for the portrait of Branigin were initially held in the Governors' Mansion. The completed portrait had many critics among the governor's friends, and was subsequently destroyed. Duckwall agreed that Branigin's casual, friendly manner was not suited to the confines of the traditional official portrait. Sittings for a second portrait were given by Branigin in the artist's studio, where a warmer light and informal atmosphere suited both the artist and her subject.

Governor Branigin is seated in a Windsor chair with legs crossed and hands resting casually, holding his glasses in his lap. The scrolled crest of the Windsor chair peeks out on either side of Branigin's head, adding a whimsical note and echoing lively facial movement. Bold brushwork and sparkling, rich color produce an animated effect which accents Branigin's pleasant personality. One feels the quality in this portrait of a happy meeting of intellectual and artistic wit.

44
ROGER D. BRANIGIN, 1967
Helen Briggs Duckwall, American*, b. 1912
oil on canvas, 44 x 36 (111.7 x 91.4)
Signed l.r.: H. B. Duckwall

Edgar D. Whitcomb, b. 1917
Governor January 13, 1969–January 9, 1973

EDGAR WHITCOMB was born in Hayden, Jennings County, Indiana. He attended Indiana University until the outbreak of World War II and then served heroically as a fighter pilot in the Philippines. His book, *Escape from Corregidor,* based on his war experiences, was published in 1958 and was popular enough to justify a paperback edition in 1967.

After the war, Whitcomb returned to Indiana University and completed his law degree. For fourteen years he practiced law in North Vernon, Seymour, and Indianapolis, developing a Republican political base. Whitcomb ran unsuccessfully for Congress in 1954 and for the Senate in 1964. In 1966, however, he was elected Indiana's secretary of state, and in 1968 he was elected governor.

A conservative Republican, Whitcomb sought the Republican nomination for United States senator in 1976 and was defeated by Richard Lugar. Since leaving office as governor, he has served as director of the Mid America World Trade Association and has resumed his law practice in Indianapolis.

* * * *

THE SEARCH for an artist to paint a portrait of Governor Whitcomb took place in the fall of 1978. This was a period of great interest in the collection inspired by the conservation treatment project of that year.[85] In response to a public announcement of the commission, fourteen individual artists and one studio applied. A committee including Governor and Mrs. Whitcomb reviewed the choices.[86] Helen M. Woodward was chosen to do the work.

Helen Woodward attended the John Herron Art Institute under William Forsyth, Clifton Wheeler, and Paul Hadley. In 1941, she studied at the Art Students' League in New York with Robert Brackman. She also was a student of Jerry Farnsworth and of Charles Hawthorne at the Cape Cod School of Art. She currently lives in Indianapolis, where she actively pursues a prestigious career as a portrait artist.

Aware of the loss of spontaneity which often accompanies the use of convenient photographic aids, this artist works only from life. Consequently, six three-hour sittings were required of Whitcomb.[87] These took place in October, 1978, at the artist's studio. Poor weather conditions caused a lack of strong daylight, so important to this artist's work, but Woodward found Whitcomb to be co-operative and interested, and the sessions were generally enjoyable. Both Governor and Mrs. Whitcomb were pleased with the result.

The governor, wearing a tan suit and striped tie, faces left and holds a white piece of paper. Behind his right shoulder is the Indiana state flag. The high-keyed festive tone of the portrait, a striking departure from the formality of most official portraiture, reflects Woodward's emphasis on vivid color relationships. Her method of painting involves the gradual buildup of color with a palette knife and the modeling of forms by the articulation of light and shade. No underdrawing in charcoal or pencil is made, and all drawn details are added as finishing touches. According to the artist, this method allows the painted image to remain more "moveable." The portrait of Governor Whitcomb is certainly animated, albeit at the expense of sound draftmanship and solid form. The figure of Whitcomb appears to emerge from the background in a kaleidoscope of brilliant color.

---

[85] A portrait of Governor Whitcomb in the collection of the Indianapolis Museum of Art was painted by Donald Mattison in 19_ for the official collection, but it was rejected by Whitcomb.

[86] "Helen M. Woodward to Paint Portrait of Governor Edgar Whitcomb," *Indiana History Bulletin,* LV, October, 1978, pp. 146–47.

[87] Interview by the editor with Helen M. Woodward, October 2_, 1978.

5
EDGAR D. WHITCOMB, 1978
Helen M. Woodward, American*, 20th century
Oil on canvas, 40 x 46 (101.6 x 116.8)
Signed l.r.: Helen M. Woodward––

Otis R. Bowen, b. 1918
Governor January 9, 1973–

OTIS BOWEN was born near Rochester, Indiana. He graduated from Indiana University and received his M.D. from Indiana University Medical School. During World War II he served in the army medical corps. When he returned to the United States he began his private practice, acquiring a respected place in Bremen as the country doctor.

For fourteen years Bowen served as a Republican representative in the state legislature, the first ever to serve three consecutive sessions as speaker of the house. Having lost the Republican nomination for governor to Edgar Whitcomb in 1968, in 1972 Bowen was elected governor. After passage of the state constitutional amendment in 1972 allowing governors to serve consecutive four-year terms, he became in 1976 the first modern governor to succeed himself. His administration has been marked by a tax restructuring program, reducing property taxes and increasing the sales tax.

Throughout his political career "Doc" Bowen has kept a prescription pad handy, recommending remedies to cure the common cold and sore throat for both colleagues and members of the press. He has also attempted to maintain the quiet, steady patience required of a physician.

* * * *

IN THEIR SEARCH for an artist to paint a portrait of Governor Bowen, the selection committee considered several prestigious contemporary American portrait painters and finally chose Everett Raymond Kinstler. In early April of 1978, soon after the terms of the commission had been arranged, Kinstler arrived in Indianapolis to meet Governor Bowen and begin the portrait.[88] Five three-hour sittings were held in a house on the grounds of the Indianapolis Museum of Art. Kinstler photographed the governor daily to aid in the completion of the portrait in his New York studio.

Although Kinstler has departed from the staid formula for executive portraiture in his representation of Governor Bowen, he has managed to invest the portrait with an imposing official air. Wearing a suit and accessories of his own choosing, the governor addresses the viewer in a relaxed, direct manner. Kinstler has caught the governor in his most characteristic gesture, with the fingertips of both hands meeting as if to emphasize a point. The background elements, a decorative molding and a carved state seal, make reference to similar ornaments found in the governor's office and lend structure and atmosphere to the picture. Kinstler's fresh approach and keen perception make the Bowen portrait an important addition to the Governors Portrait Collection.

A protégé of James Montgomery Flagg, the famed illustrator and creator of the image of Uncl Sam for a World War I recruiting poster, Kinstle worked as an illustrator of books, comic books and magazines for fifteen years. Study with th Indiana-born portrait artist Wayman Adam sparked Kinstler's interest in portraiture, to whic he turned with increasing enthusiasm in the lat 1950s. Since 1963, the artist has received man important commissions, including portraits c twenty-five United States cabinet officers, al painted from life. Most recently Kinstler has com pleted the official portrait of President Geral Ford. A National Academician, Kinstler is a active member of several arts organizations includ ing the American Watercolor Society and the Na tional Arts Club.

[88] Everett Raymond Kinstler to editor, September 1, 1978. Fi pertaining to Governors' portraits, Indianapolis Museum of Art.

46
OTIS R. BOWEN, 1978
Everett Raymond Kinstler, American, b. 1927
oil on canvas, 40 x 34 (101.6 x 86.4)
Signed and dated at l.r.: ©/EVERETT RAYMOND KINSTLER/1978

Governors, in order of their terms

1. William Henry Harrison (1773–1841)
   May 13, 1800–December 28, 1812

2. John Gibson (1740–1822)
   July 4, 1800–January 10, 1801
   June, 1812–May, 1813

3. Thomas Posey (1750–1818)
   March 3, 1813–November 7, 1816

4. Jonathan Jennings (1784–1834)
   November 7, 1816–September 12, 1822

5. Ratliff Boon (1781–1844)
   September 12–December 5, 1822

6. William Hendricks (1782–1850)
   December 5, 1822–February 12, 1825

7. James Brown Ray (1794–1848)
   February 12, 1825–December 7, 1831

8. Noah Noble (1794–1844)
   December 7, 1831–December 6, 1837

9. David Wallace (1799–1859)
   December 6, 1837–December 9, 1840

10. Samuel Bigger (1802–1846)
    December 9, 1840–December 6, 1843

11. James Whitcomb (1795–1852)
    December 6, 1843–December 26, 1848

12. Paris Chipman Dunning (1806–1884)
    December 26, 1848–December 5, 1849

13. Joseph Albert Wright (1810–1867)
    December 5, 1849–January 12, 1857

14. Ashbel Parsons Willard (1820–1860)
    January 12, 1857–October 4, 1860

15. Abram Adams Hammond (1814–1874)
    October 4, 1860–January 14, 1861

16. Henry Smith Lane (1811–1881)
    January 14–16, 1861

17. Oliver Perry Morton (1823–1877)
    January 16, 1861–January 23, 1867

18. Conrad Baker (1817–1885)
    January 23, 1867–January 13, 1873

19. Thomas Andrews Hendricks (1819–1885)
    January 13, 1873–January 8, 1877

20. James Douglas Williams (1808–1880)
    January 8, 1877–November 20, 1880

21. Isaac Pusey Gray (1825–1895)
    November 20, 1880–January 10, 1881
    January 12, 1885–January 14, 1889

22. Albert Gallatin Porter (1824–1897)
    January 10, 1881–January 12, 1885

23. Alvin Peterson Hovey (1821–1891)
    January 14, 1899–November 23, 1891

24. Ira Joy Chase (1834–1895)
    November 23, 1891–Janaury 9, 1893

25. Claude Matthews (1845–1898)
    January 9, 1893–January 11, 1897

26. James Atwell Mount (1843–1901)
    January 11, 1897–January 14, 1901

27. Winfield Taylor Durbin (1847–1928)
    January 14, 1901–January 9, 1905

28. James Frank Hanly (1863–1920)
    January 9, 1905–January 11, 1909

29. Thomas Riley Marshall (1854–1925)
    January 11, 1909–January 13, 1913

30. Samuel Moffett Ralston (1857–1925)
    January 13, 1913–January 8, 1917

31. James Putnam Goodrich (1864–1940)
    January 8, 1917–January 10, 1921

32. Warren Terry McCray (1865–1938)
    January 10, 1921–April 30, 1924

33. Emmett Forrest Branch (1874–1932)
    April 30, 1924–January 12, 1925

34. Edward L. Jackson (1873–1954)
    January 12, 1925–January 14, 1929

35. Harry Guyer Leslie (1878–1937)
    January 14, 1929–January 9, 1933

36. Paul Vories McNutt (1891–1955)
    January 9, 1933–January 11, 1937

37. Maurice Clifford Townsend (1884–1954)
    January 11, 1937–January 13, 1941

38. Henry Frederick Schricker (1883–1966)
    January 13, 1941–January 8, 1945

39. Ralph F. Gates (1893–1978)
    January 8, 1945–January 10, 1949

40. Henry Frederick Schricker (1883–1966)
    January 10, 1949–January 12, 1953

41. George N. Craig (b. 1909)
    January 12, 1953–January 14, 1957

42. Harold W. Handley (1909–1972)
    January 14, 1957–January 9, 1961

43. Matthew E. Welsh (b. 1912)
    January 9, 1961–January 11, 1965

44. Roger D. Branigin (1902–1975)
    January 11, 1965–January 13, 1969

45. Edgar D. Whitcomb (b. 1917)
    January 13, 1969–January 9, 1973

46. Otis R. Bowen (b. 1918)
    January 9, 1973–

ditor's Note: In the following appendices, num-
ers in bold face indicate the catalogue number of
e portrait in the collection. Numbers in light
ce indicate the page in this publication where
e respective catalogue entries begin.

Artists and Subjects

Governors Alphabetically